Marketing

Marketing

A guide to the fundamentals

Patrick Forsyth

Bloomberg Press
New York

THE ECONOMIST IN ASSOCIATION WITH PROFILE BOOKS LTD

This edition published in the United States and Canada by Bloomberg Press
Published in the U.K. by Profile Books Ltd, 2009

Printed in Canada

1 3 5 7 9 10 8 6 4 2

Library of Congress Cataloging-in-Publication Data on file

ISBN 978-1-57660-329-1

Contents

Introduction

They say that if you build a better mousetrap than your neighbour, people are going to come running. They are like hell! It's marketing that makes the difference.

Ed Johnson

Marketing is one of the most misunderstood business disciplines. Too often it is assumed to be just one aspect of what it involves, such as advertising. Its full extent is often underestimated and misunderstood by people in other areas of the business, yet marketing is a specialist activity that influences the success of any organisation.

It has been said that marketing is too important to leave to marketing people. Certainly its effects are wide ranging and many people are involved in it, influence it (albeit obliquely) or are affected by it.

This book explains and demystifies marketing. Its main aim is to explain marketing to non-marketing people so that marketing and other functions and activities will work better together because they will understand each other better. It is also aimed at those directly involved in marketing, including experienced marketers, who may find it helpful to be reminded of the fundamentals.

In explaining marketing (and its jargon) this book uses a variety of examples to illustrate its content. These are common examples familiar to many people, though they range widely and may be from organisations large and small in a variety of markets. The language is deliberately general. For instance, purchasers are referred to as customers, though a service organisation such as a firm of accountants would probably talk about clients and a hotel would call them guests. Similarly, a product may well be a service but the word product is often used to encompass both.

The book has four parts. The first two chapters (part 1) explain the complexity of marketing so that readers understand the role of the various elements and how they fit and work together. The overall premise of marketing and its components is essentially common sense. Having this broad picture in mind will make sure that as the different, and disparate, elements and techniques of marketing are outlined in parts 2-4, the reader will more easily appreciate them and how they contribute to the marketing function.

Marketing people and marketing activity intend to create success and profitability. Organisations in which everyone understands the importance of marketing (and their role in it) to business success generally relate better to their marketplace than those with a weaker marketing culture. Everyone is more likely to play a full part and the organisation will be more successful in contending with an increasingly competitive world.

1

Overview

1 Marketing in context

If we are not customer driven, our cars won't be either.

Attributed to a Ford Motor Company marketer

Marketing is one of the most misunderstood areas of business. Despite organisations becoming increasingly marketing-focused, marketers often find that wrong assumptions are made about their role. Others do not have this problem. People know that the production manager keeps the production line moving, quality control speaks for itself, the accountant keeps the score, and so on. But marketing is often thought to be no more than advertising or selling. This mistaken perception matters because so many people in an organisation are (wittingly or not) a part of its marketing or affected by it. Many influence its effectiveness, from top to bottom of an organisation, across its departments and functions, so it is crucial that marketing is not an isolated function but widely understood so that everyone can play their part and make marketing effective in its role of "bringing in the business".

What is marketing?

There are many definitions of marketing. The UK's Chartered Institute of Marketing says it is "the management process responsible for identifying, anticipating and satisfying customer requirement profitably". Philip Kotler, an American marketing guru, has defined it thus:

Marketing is the business function that identifies current unfulfilled needs and wants, defines and measures their magnitude, determines which target markets the organisation can best serve, and decides on appropriate products, services, and programmes to serve these markets. Thus marketing serves as the link between a society's needs and its pattern of industrial response.

These two definitions express the complexity involved and make it clear that marketing is more than just the "marketing department". The late Peter Drucker, a leading management thinker, however, was content to say: "Marketing is looking at the business through the customers' eyes." Indeed, everything stems from that.

Marketing has five descriptions:

▶ A concept that the customer is of prime importance. Success comes from seeing every aspect of the business through the eyes of customers, anticipating their needs and supplying what they want in a way they like; not simply trying to sell whatever someone has decided should be produced. This is no more than common sense. In different businesses "customers" encompass a number of different people or, in the case of business-to-business (B2B) marketing, organisations. Regardless of whether products or services are sold direct to the public or through agents, wholesalers and retailers, all organisations do best by embracing the marketing concept and demonstrating an intention to serve their customers.

▶ A function responsible for identifying, anticipating and satisfying customer requirements profitably, and which therefore is concerned with the process that implements the concept. This function must be directed from a senior level and take a broad view of the business. Someone must wear the marketing "hat", even if that person has other responsibilities as well. Whoever is involved and however matters are arranged, the final responsibility must be clear and sufficient time must be found to carry it out.

▶ A range of techniques, including not just selling and advertising but also market research, product development, pricing, presentation and promotion (which encompasses advertising, merchandising, direct mail, public relations and sales promotion).

▶ A process that acts to "bring in the business" by using various techniques continuously, appropriately and creatively to make success more certain. Marketing cannot guarantee success, nor can it be applied by rote. The skill of those involved in marketing lies in precisely how they act in an area that is rightly referred to as being as much an art as a science.

▶ A system that takes into account both internal and external factors, many of which restrict what can be done or achieved. The marketing system links customers and potential customers with the company and attempts to reconcile any conflicts between them, such as the organisation's goal to maximise profits and the potential customer's desire to get the best value for money. (See Chapter 2.)

The marketing process

Marketing is a continuous process, as shown in Figure 1.1.

▶ Market research attempts to identify and anticipate consumer needs; what people want, how they want it supplied, and whether they may want it differently in the future. Research can analyse the past and review current attitudes but it cannot predict, so it must concentrate on trends and be interpreted carefully. Even so, it can help to reduce risk and aid innovation and can be used throughout the marketing process as well as in the early stages.

▶ Forecasting is necessary in trying to discover what quantity of a product or service may be purchased in the future. Identifying a need is of little use commercially if only a handful of people have that need. As Neils Bohr, a Nobel Prize-winning physicist, said: "Prediction is never easy. Especially of the future." Forecasting is never 100% accurate, but the best possible estimate is needed to aid planning and reduce risk.

▶ Product and/or service development is, for most businesses, a continuous process. Sometimes the process is more evolution than revolution – note the regularity with which car manufacturers upgrade model specifications. Sometimes changes are more cosmetic than real. A new "improved" floor cleaner

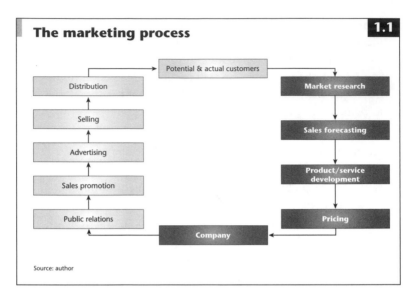

The marketing process   1.1

Source: author

with ingredient X may leave customers hardly able to perceive a difference, yet still communicate a feeling of added value. Sometimes change is so rapid – as with computers and other high-tech products – that consumers become frustrated when the model they have bought is rapidly superseded by a new one. But in today's highly competitive world, no organisation can afford not to be innovative in the products or services it offers customers or in the way it markets them.

▶ Price is a marketing variable and must be set carefully, as must pricing policy. This is not only to make sure that financial objectives are met, but also to create an appropriate feeling of value for money among customers and potential customers.

▶ External promotion is crucial to let potential customers know clearly and persuasively what is available and to encourage them to buy. It involves a variety of techniques, such as advertising, direct mail, sales promotion and public relations, which can be used together or separately. Brands and products depend on visibility for success. Nobody can buy something they do not know exists; products grow into market leaders largely because of the promotional investment made in them.

▶ Selling involves personal communication and often forms a final, crucial, link in the chain that connects a company to its market.

▶ Distribution is the system that delivers products and services into the marketplace or direct to the customer. It can make all the difference to a product's success. Marketing sometimes involves a direct relationship: for example, the product is sent direct to the customer as a response to an advertisement. More often, however, there is a chain of intermediaries, as in the case of consumer products, which usually go from a manufacturer to a retailer, perhaps via a wholesaler, before being bought by a customer. In a poorly managed distribution system there may be too many products stocked in one place and too few in another, resulting in lost sales. The distribution system also needs to be able to cope with changes in seasonal demand.

Organisational functions and resources

Every company has three basic functions (which when well directed operate in a co-ordinated fashion) and two major resources. The three basic functions are:

▶ production (which in a service industry relates to what people do, for example auditing or writing software);

▶ finance;

▶ marketing.

The two major resources are:

▶ capital;

▶ labour.

Each function has different tasks and different objectives, often operates on a different timescale, attracts different types of people and regards money in a different way. So, although they all contribute towards the same company objectives, there is likely to be some internal conflict between, say, marketing and production (on how much should be produced and how much is likely to be sold), or marketing and finance (on what one says needs to be spent and what the other says can be afforded).

The marketing culture has a significant effect on the success of an organisation's marketing. It refers to the way in which marketing activity is supported and assisted by the attitudes and activities of people who are not part of the marketing department but whose work influences success in the marketplace.

Thus people at every level need to understand each other and work together so that the organisation operates coherently and effectively. Those dealing with customers either face to face or by telephone have a big influence on what customers and potential customers think of an organisation and whether they will want to do business with it. First Direct, the UK internet and telephone banking arm of HSBC, has a high reputation for the way its employees deal with customers. This helps the bank to retain existing customers and also, through recommendation, attract new ones. Indeed, so powerful can this effect be that First Direct was shown by a GFK Financial Research Survey in 2008 to have 89% of customers rating its service "exceptional or very satisfactory", while 38% of its new customers come directly from recommendation. Some firms, however, have call centres or helplines that irritate their customers – and drive them into the hands of competing businesses. A Citizens Advice survey in 2008 showed that customers were least satisfied with UK utility companies in this respect; more than one-third of people had to wait for more than 30 minutes to get to speak to someone.

Profits are only generated externally, and a business must be organised in a way that allows marketing to be market oriented. Customers care nothing for internal inconvenience or confusion; they judge on external image. Things done for internal reasons but which do not work in the marketplace are likely to reduce the effectiveness of marketing – and may cause serious damage.

The marketing-led approach to business has predominated since the 1970s and increasing competition has made it more important. It has had to become more sophisticated and more focused on activity designed to differentiate products and services from the competition.

The marketing mix

The marketing mix describes the variables that marketers must work with in deciding their strategy. It describes the elements of marketing that must be organised successfully to create an effective strategic approach: These are the "three Ps":

▶ product (or service);

▶ price;

▶ presentation (or promotion).

All are important and are referred to throughout this book. However, product is discussed in detail in Chapter 3, pricing in Chapter 4 and presentation in Chapters 10–12.

A fourth P is place, which links markets and distribution (see Chapter 6), and recently marketers have referred to the "seven Ps". The extra Ps are people, physical evidence and process.

People encompasses everyone at every stage of marketing activity, both inside and outside the company; it covers customers, employees and suppliers. For instance, waiters are a major influence on restaurant customers. Similarly, everyone in both the supply chain (such as parts suppliers) and the distribution chain must be satisfied with their relationship and work well together if marketing is to maximise success. The more influence marketing can bring to bear on people, the greater the potential level of market success. It is important to consider:

▶ individuals' attitudes and how they influence performance;

▶ the quality of the motivational environment that keeps people productive;

▶ the skills people need and any training required.

Physical evidence describes the tangible aspects of delivering a product to customers. For example, merchandising and display techniques contribute to the convenience and visual impact of products in shops and make purchase more likely.

Process includes using bar codes for product tracking and identification, using loyalty cards to track and analyse customers' spending habits, or processing a customer's credit card at the time of purchase. Two things are crucial: accuracy and convenience. Customers become upset if they are charged an incorrect amount and they expect all processes involved with buying a product purchase to be quick and convenient.

Key points

▶ Marketing is central to an organisation and its relationship with its customers and potential customers.

▶ It is a creative process, based on science, but does not guarantee success.

▶ Customers can be fickle and unpredictable; marketing carries a real element of risk.

▶ Successful marketing produces profit.

▶ Marketing works best when people across all functions understand and are involved in the marketing approach.

Marketing realities

The business has two – and only two –
basic functions: marketing and innovation.
Marketing and innovation produce results: all
the rest are costs.

Peter Drucker, management guru

Businesses do not operate in a world where all they have to do is find a product people want, make it and tell people about it. Many external factors must be taken into account if marketing is to be successful.

External factors

Marketing operates in an environment that may either restrict or assist it. Among the restrictions that marketers must consider are the following:

▶ Total demand. This varies, but it is always finite. More people buy razor blades than buy footballs, and footballs last longer too. Discovering the potential for any product is part of market identification and research, and marketing plans must always reflect this area of ultimate restriction.

▶ Availability of capital and labour. Marketing costs money, as does making a product. Ultimately, a business needs to make an acceptable return on its investment. Labour costs money too, and a business needs the right number of people with the right skills if it is to succeed. Providing technical service support to marketing is just one example of where many specialist staff may be needed. Talented people help to make marketing work, but too few of them dilutes its effectiveness.

▶ Competition. If competitor A sells more, the market often shrinks for competitor B; if someone has a Fuji camera, do they want a Canon as well? Competition laws exist to prevent monopolies or one company holding too much market power in a specific sector. But competition also reflects people's spending patterns and so also comes from other types of products. For example, books compete with other leisure products such as films or DVDs – and book purchases come from discretionary income and so also compete with essential purchases such as replacements for worn-out clothes. Sheaffer pens compete with Cross (which differentiates by giving a lifetime guarantee), but also with ballpoint pens, pencils and computers. If a house needs painting, the owner may not be able to afford a holiday as well, so the paint competes with travel spending. Similarly, Coca-Cola has a one-third share of the global soft drinks market, but its percentage share of the broader beverage market is a small single figure.

▶ Legislation. New laws and regulations are introduced while existing ones are modified and often tightened up. Marketers need to look ahead; what sales will be affected by extra restrictions, and might such changes expand any other market? When the UK government banned smoking in public places in 2007, JD Wetherspoon, a large chain of bars, estimated that as a result sales fell by 1% in the following three months. At the same time, sales of nicotine gum to help people stop smoking increased by 2%. Responding positively to legislation can strengthen marketing; laws designed to improve car safety provide marketers with an incentive to demonstrate that their company's cars are the safest, even if they also want to promote other attributes, such as comfort, speed and status.

▶ Supply of raw materials. It is important to predict (as far as possible) the price and availability of raw materials. Commodity prices increased rapidly as demand from China rose. Similarly, oil-price fluctuations affect the cost of transporting raw materials long distances. Supply is also crucial; for example, the weather affects the quantities of food products available for sale.

▶ Channels of distribution. The lack of a distributor in a potentially rich export market will limit overall sales, but this is easily recognised and can be remedied.

▶ Technology. The impossible is impossible until it becomes possible, and the state of technology may prevent something being done, at least for the moment. But as technology advances, new products arrive and markets change.

Some factors are comparatively easy to work with while others are truly external. Some have a long-term effect rather than creating short-term shifts. All can have a direct impact on markets and marketing opportunities – for good or ill. One change can produce both: for example, a legal change about testing medicines might delay the launch of new drugs and reduce the revenues of pharmaceutical companies such as Eli Lilly or Merck at the same time as boosting the profits gained from different treatments, including alternatives such as homeopathy.

Other external influences that may create opportunities and limitations include the following:

▶ Social. Demographic trends or lifestyle changes affect markets. For example, in families where both partners go out to work, there are a greater opportunities for convenience foods, and the increase in affluent retired people has created opportunities for travel firms.

▶ Political. Changes in government bring about changes in legislation, such as health and safety laws that affect product design, and new consumer rights may affect the information that can or must be given about products. Government decisions can also help to open new markets through the establishment of free-trade zones; however, extra import tariffs will diminish the attractiveness of a market for exporters. Such decisions are often political, even if they are taken ostensibly for reasons of economic policy.

▶ Economic. Changes in indirect taxes such as sales tax affect the price of goods and services, which may in turn affect demand. Changes in direct taxes such as income tax affect people's incomes and therefore what they have available to spend, as do changes in interest rates for those who have savings or mortgages. Economic policy has a fundamental impact on the business environment and although governments and central banks seek to direct it in an orderly fashion, market forces have a substantial role in determining it.

▶ Technology. The internet and e-mail have created new product opportunities and new ways to market products. The web has revolutionised retailing, increasing price transparency and diminishing the number of city-centre travel agents. The ability to download digital files to mobile phones and devices such as Apple's iPod has radically changed the business of music publishing, while the ease of attaching document files to e-mails has revolutionised methods of communication, reducing the market for postal services and sending the fax machine market into meltdown.

Any area of considerable and continuing change presents both opportunities and threats. An organisation must monitor the market and anticipate how it might change so that it can turn potential opportunities to its advantage and act to minimise the damage from threats. Some changes have both positive and negative effects; for example, when Singapore banned the sale of chewing gum the global market decreased, but other confectionery products may have benefited.

Many organisations separate the everyday work of marketing today's products from work on future projects. Unless sufficient time and human and other resources are deployed in exploration and analysis (and in some industries, extensive and technical research and development) as a separate activity, the pressures of securing current revenue can distract and lead to opportunities being missed or dangers catching marketers unawares. For example, it took the established Swiss watchmakers years (and thousands of lost jobs) to turn electronic after the success of East Asian manufacturers in the 1960s and 1970s, and it was only in 1983 that a Swiss firm launched Swatch.

These kinds of influence have general effects and also affect narrow sectors. For example, the trend of getting older younger (GOY) has made many traditional toys redundant at a much younger age for today's children than in the past; conversely, other products are becoming more appealing to younger age groups. Building blocks give way to computer games and product opportunities change. Marketing must both respond to and deal with such factors; it can also encourage or even trigger them.

The life and death of products

The product life-cycle reflects the way in which a product performs from its inception and launch to such time as declining sales may lead to its being discontinued.

No product or service remains successful forever. Some fashion products are here today and gone tomorrow. Research shows that whether a product's life is short or long, over time the overall pattern is similar: a bell shaped curve. Usually this is divided into five classic stages – introduction, growth, maturity, decline and phase out:

▶ Introduction is a period of often slow growth in which profits are almost non existent because of the costs of development and launch.

▶ Growth is a period of more rapid market acceptance and substantial profit improvement.

▶ Maturity is a period of potential slowdown in sales growth because the product has achieved acceptance by most of the potential buyers. Profits peak in this period and may start to decline because of the increased marketing expenditure needed to sustain the product's position against competition. Much marketing activity is aimed at maintaining products at this peak and extending their life. For example, 3M's Scotch tape was launched in 1952 and Lego building blocks in the 1930s; Kellogg's Corn Flakes are more than 100 years old. These brands (and many others) have needed constant refreshment to reinvigorate them.

▶ Decline is the period when sales drift downwards and profits are eroded.

▶ Phase out is the final period during which the product is withdrawn or changed so radically that it enters a new life-cycle. Eventually everything reaches this stage. For example, Polaroid instant cameras, which first appeared in 1947, were discontinued in 2008 in the face of competition from the digital camera.

Deciding when each stage begins and ends is somewhat arbitrary. Usually, they are based on where the rate of sales growth or decline becomes pronounced. Not all products pass through the bell shaped product life-cycle. Some grow rapidly from the very beginning, effectively skipping the introductory stage: others go directly from introduction to maturity. Some products move from maturity to a second period of rapid growth.

Customers and the cycle

The product life-cycle is a fact, so marketers must work with it to best effect. When a new product is launched, they must take steps to stimulate awareness, interest, trial and purchase. This can take time, and in the introductory stage only a few people (innovators) may buy. If the product is good, larger numbers of buyers (early adopters) are drawn in. Competitors entering the market speed up the adoption process by increasing the market's awareness and putting downward pressure on prices. More buyers come in (early majority) as the product gains acceptance. Eventually, the rate of growth decreases as the number of potential new buyers approaches zero and sales stabilise at the replacement purchase rate. Without action they will decline as newer products appear and divert the interest of buyers from the existing product. Figure 2.1 summarises this process.

Some well-known products have been around for a long time. Some are maintained through modification, effectively starting their cycle again at its peak; others remain much the same for long periods. For example, Nestlé's Black Magic chocolates were launched in the 1930s and not a single flavour was changed for more than 50 years. Others products go into the doldrums, sometimes for years, but

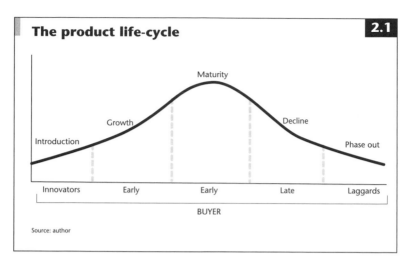

The product life-cycle   2.1

Maturity

Growth   Decline

Introduction   Phase out

| Innovators | Early | Early | Late | Laggards |

BUYER

Source: author

are revived, such as Brylcreem hair styling products and Lucozade energy and sports drinks; still others disappear without trace, such as Ford's Edsel, which no one liked. Even the mighty Coca-Cola dropped the reformulation of "New" Coke after customers rejected it. This is the product life-cycle at work, and the more long-lived products are usually a sign of successful marketing.

Launching a product is a major task – it is commonly estimated that as many as 9 out of 10 new products fail in a short time, especially in the fast-moving consumer goods (FMCG) category, which includes items such as soap and grocery products. Beyond that, most marketing activity is directed to fit the product's position in the life-cycle. The marketing for a mature product is designed to maintain it at its peak, using techniques designed to keep existing users buying regularly and to attract new customers, each separate in the details of how they work.

Social and ethical considerations

Marketing is a force in the world. It can do good by helping consumers, providing choice and, in its social marketing guise (everything from charities to government road safety campaigns), seeking to right wrongs and make changes for the better. But it may also do harm. If a product's packaging, when discarded, harms the environment, should the producer be prepared to spend more to avoid the problem? If a company's advertising offends some people (as Benetton did in the early 1990s with its advertising featuring AIDS sufferers) but boosts sales, should it be changed even if to do so would jeopardise the higher level of sales that had been achieved? Benetton stuck to its guns; but in Singapore the volume of protest meant the cosmetics brand Lookin' Good for Jesus was discontinued almost as soon as it was launched. The YouTube website, which targets young people, has been criticised for displaying advertisements for alcoholic drinks.

Taking the moral high ground poses many questions, for instance:

▶ Will customers notice the change?

▶ What will customers think about a change?

▶ What are the costs and how will it affect profitability?

▶ What will competitors do?

And, ultimately, what will be the effect on the business of one course of action rather than another?

Marketers must take such factors into account in deciding how they do things. It is not always easy to get it right; breaches of advertising codes are sometimes a case of sailing too close to the wind and the line is not easy to judge (except with hindsight). The effects of getting such decisions wrong are clear:

▶ Illegal action will result in penalties.

▶ Breaching industry and other codes can result in sanctions.

▶ Any action that consumers disapprove of can result in bad publicity, as firms such as Gap and Nike discovered when it was revealed that some of their overseas suppliers were using cheap child labour. This can hit sales or even lead to a boycott.

The reverse is also true. Organisations clearly making determined attempts to be ethical can attract good publicity and enjoy extra sales as a result. For example, many products are promoted to stress their "green" attributes (though if such claims are spurious or overstated, this can do more harm than good). A growing number of organisations are at pains to be seen to be taking a manifestly ethical approach as a main platform of their offering; the UK's

Co-operative Bank and certain investment funds are examples (the SocialFunds.com website covers socially responsible investing in the United States). Social and ethical issues affect consumers' attitudes in many ways and are important considerations for marketers.

Market segmentation

Size matters

Markets are not one amorphous whole of everyone who buys a particular product. They divide into parts, or market segments. A market segment is a group of people for whom the product, and all its benefits, is suitable. It is part of a larger market that may be selected as a discrete target, in which potential customers have a recognisable profile.

What is a market?

A market is a large collection of people somewhere in the world. Companies have to inform these people about what they can offer them and how it will suit them. However, some (possibly most) may have no interest in the product and so are not part of the target market.

Organisations must clearly identify those who might be interested in their products. Only then can they use precise marketing to influence potential customers. Consequently, a market segment is a group of people for whom a product, and all its benefits, is suitable.

Whatever is on sale, many people (the market) may buy, but not all will do so for the same reason or purpose. Thus any market can be broken down into smaller markets or segments and ultimately into niche markets – the smallest manifestation of a segment. Niche markets, although they may be small, can be highly profitable and represent the ultimate in customer identification. The foundation for effective marketing exists only once markets have been identified and market knowledge has been built up.

The motor industry is a good example of segmentation in action. People buy cars for reasons that include status, carrying capacity and economy. Ultimately, the division is specific. If someone wants a family-sized car and has economy and status in mind, a more economical yet undistinguished car will not appeal. People who are in one segment will not necessarily move to another. By definition, a segment is a group of actual and potential customers with the same needs that can be satisfied by similar products.

Even in "mass markets", such as those for soap or soup, customers will buy for different reasons and uses. If these different uses can be identified, "cherry picking" or market specialisation can take place to create extra profit. For example, many biological detergents sell more on the special characteristic of removing stains than on general cleaning criteria. However, not all market segments work alongside each other – would a Porsche pick-up truck have the same appeal as a Porsche car? – so many companies specialise, focusing their efforts on a selection of segments. There are even segments for products such as industrial equipment and components and for services such as accountants and hotels. American Express tailors its products with various types of card including gold and platinum.

How big must a segment or niche be? The group of potential customers must be sufficiently large to define and make it worthwhile to target with a tailored marketing approach. Ultimately, it is a question of cost and return rather than the number of potential customers.

A segment must:

▶ be homogeneous (containing people sufficiently similar, at least in terms of their needs, to work as a group that is different from others);

▶ be large enough to exploit;

▶ have potential that can be quantified and qualified;

▶ be accessible within a given cost or timeframe.

There are many examples of incorrectly defined businesses. Shops selling running shoes, tracksuits and associated athletic wear have been known to define their business as providing athletic apparel and thus target runners and athletes. But not only runners and athletes buy and wear clothes from such shops; much of what they sell may be worn by people who wish to be fashionable or who simply want to wear comfortable leisure clothing. Even an apparently simple market consists of segments, in this case at least two – runners and athletes, and a more general sector – and probably more.

It is crucial for organisations to correctly identify the business they are in and relate it to the characteristics of the market(s) involved. This means that they should be able to correctly identify their potential customers, at whom marketing efforts can be directed, which will make sure that resources such as time, money and effort are used efficiently. Carefully considering the composition and characteristics of potential markets creates a greater chance of success.

Markets may be small and local or worldwide:

▶ Exporting implies that goods or services are marketed and delivered from one country to another.

▶ International marketing implies that the producing company has a presence overseas through joint ventures, subsidiary companies or overseas offices and factories.

Action related to market segmentation

The concept of segmentation presents a number of different possibilities and scales of action for marketing approaches, including the following:

▶ Mass marketing. All buyers are considered as the same. This has the advantage of economies of scale and reducing costs. However, the "one size fits all" concept is difficult to sustain in a world of increasing customisation and differentiation. Many organisations have moved away from mass marketing. Even Coca-Cola, which was originally available only in one size of bottle, has for many years been available in a number of types and sizes of container as well as a number of different variations. This helps it to appeal to different market segments. Even the world's largest "one product brand", Wrigley, offers many flavours and types of chewing gum.

▶ Segment marketing. Normally the target is a large identifiable group within a market that has an attribute that differentiates it from the mass. The differences may not be great but they are discernible, and therefore different consumers can have a product or service that more closely meets their needs. So-called supermini cars, such as Volkswagen's Golf GT, comprise one market segment.

▶ Niche marketing. This targets a small group whose needs are not being well served. Often these groups will pay a premium price for the benefit received. So high-performance superminis, a small proportion of the supermini segment, form a niche market.

▶ Local marketing. The benefits being offered reflect the character of the region or location being served. This could be a place where there is only one of a particular type of business.

▶ Individual marketing. Also known as one-to-one marketing and micro marketing, this offers customised products to meet an individual's exact needs. For example, Volvo can customise a car from its range with the choice of about 4,000 combinations of colour, engine, trim and so on. Dell markets its computers in a similar way.

How segmentation helps

Segmenting a market requires careful thought and analysis. This uses resources, so the benefits must be identifiable and worthwhile financially. Organisations should be able to:

▶ Compare marketing opportunities. This can reveal gaps in the market where a particular benefit is not readily available from other suppliers. Therefore, the attributes required could be offered to that particular segment to fill the perceived gap. Marketers must make sure that the segment is large enough to provide an adequate return on the investment.

▶ Allocate the marketing budget effectively. The aim is to concentrate expenditure on markets that will provide the highest return. This helps to prevent the marketing effort being wasted on products for which in particular markets there is little demand or where it is not possible to offer them competitively.

▶ Make adjustments. It may only be necessary to modify one aspect of the mix to make it more appealing to a chosen segment.

Addressing market segments helps to make sure that marketing achieves the organisation's objectives. This can only be done if:

▶ The characteristics of the individual market are known.

▶ The influence of specific buying groups upon those markets is understood.

▶ Promotional activity is directed towards the specific market segments.

▶ These segments are exploited to achieve the defined marketing objectives.

Splitting markets into smaller segments makes marketing better able to maximise the return on an investment.

Key points

Marketing involves:

▶ taking the realities of the situation properly into account in plans and actions;

▶ monitoring actual and anticipating likely external changes so as to be able to take action to help marketing to succeed;

▶ understanding the markets in which the business operates – this may demand research and analysis of the information it produces;

▶ choosing products well and setting prices carefully; customers and competitors give no quarter to ill-conceived ventures;

▶ making time for creative and systematic thought, analysis and formulating a clear plan of action.

2

The marketing process

"Product" considerations

While great devices are invented in the laboratory, great products are invented in the marketing department.

William H. Davidow, former vice-president, strategy, Intel

Marketing is a complex process involving many disparate activities. These activities all depend on the product, but what is the "product" exactly? All products were once new, even if the likes of Club Med, Swatch and Federal Express now seem ubiquitous. Many products are well known; those that are said to be iconic range from instant coffee to the iPhone. Products change over time – note the way that Nokia and others have extended the capabilities of the mobile phone. Once the size of a brick and only able to make phone calls, it has progressively shrunk and added a camera, as well as the ability to surf the internet and play music and film.

Furthermore, the nature of a product or service directs the kind of marketing approaches that must back it. Marketing canned soup to families is clearly different from marketing it to hotel chains. Compare this with Boeing selling jet airliners to airlines. These are just two examples, but the circumstances involved are chalk and cheese; every product demands its own specific kind of marketing.

This chapter explores the different marketing approaches to different products and the choices involved in applying them. The term brand applies both to an individual product, such as a Mars bar, and to a range of products that may be linked together (here including Mars ice cream). Brands can be powerful and worldwide

– for example, Sony, IBM and Ford – and product ranges can be huge, so much so that they can get out of hand. In 1999 Unilever sold more than 1,800 products under its portfolio of brands including Knorr, Hellman's, Flora, Vaseline, Dove, Omo, Domestos, Surf and Lipton's; a process of rationalisation is continuing with the target of reducing to a few hundred products still some way off.

The way marketing activity is planned and deployed is largely determined by the nature of the "product" and of the producer organisation.

Consumer goods

Consumer goods are anything bought by individual shoppers from cars and refrigerators to clothes; fast-moving consumer goods (FMCG) are items bought repeatedly to replace earlier purchases such as soap and toothpaste.

Consumer goods marketing is the most familiar part of marketing. It is what many people think of when the word marketing is mentioned, remembering strong product slogans, such as Gillette's "The best a man can get", or "My goodness, my Guinness", which was coined in the 1930s by novelist Dorothy L. Sayers. It is characterised by being:

▶ highly visible – these are products seen everywhere;

▶ directed at large markets – almost everyone is a customer for toothpaste;

▶ promoted in many media – from television advertising to advertisements in glossy magazines or on the web;

▶ backed by large budgets, especially for promotion – which are necessary to reach the large markets and do so repeatedly;

▶ highly competitive – in many product areas there are many companies making essentially similar products (though small differences do matter in the marketplace);

▶ reliant on the creation of a brand image – that is, the product or service, the name and the whole "personality" that goes with it;

▶ creative in approach – the style of many consumer

advertisements is often the idea of the advertising agencies used to plan and organise promotional campaigns.

In marketing consumer goods many large firms have a string of brand names, all of which need marketing. Sometimes this is apparent, as with the many products marketed under, say, the Nestlé name. Other companies use a variety of different brand names and the association with the main company is not featured strongly, as with Unilever. Multiple brands and wide product ranges require product managers who are in effect marketing managers for a single brand rather than a whole organisation (an approach pioneered by Procter & Gamble in the 1920s). Given the scale of marketing often involved, these are big jobs with the challenging task of achieving and maintaining a certain level of market share – the amount of a product sold as a percentage of total sales of similar products (which implies that the total sales of the particular product, instant coffee or whatever, is known).

Those people marketing consumer goods are in the heartland of the marketing world. It is a sophisticated form of marketing that utilises the full panoply of marketing techniques, though competitive pressures and the challenge of making anything successful in the marketplace are just as real whatever the product.

Industrial products

Industrial goods are those sold to industry rather than the general public. The range includes machine tools and the items they are used to make or products necessary to them (such as spare parts) as well as a whole range of components. On a larger scale, industrial products include anything from ships to aircraft. They also include products resulting from derived demand (see below).

The characteristics of industrial product marketing are:

▶ an inherently smaller number of potential customers – everyone may need toothpaste, but relatively few need an industrial lathe;

▶ long lead times as products are designed and engineered – a new car may take four or five years to produce and a new aircraft much longer;

Derived demand

Derived demand exists, for example, in a company making and selling glass bottles. If a brewer decides to launch a new beer, it will collaborate with the glass company about the bottle's design to produce an attractive image and sell the beer, but the success of the beer will dictate how many bottles are sold. This is a routine part of marketing activity in some fields. Another example is Intel, which sells to computer manufacturers, but advertises to consumers to influence them to buy machines containing its processing chips.

▶ "professional buyers" – often people paid to buy and trained to get the deal they want;

▶ people working in it may need a technical background, qualification or understanding related to the products they are marketing;

▶ more specialist and targeted approaches – advertising heat exchangers on television would be expensive and poorly targeted, but advertisements in technical journals also need to be cost effective;

▶ personal selling – this is likely to have an important role as the final link in the chain often depends on a good personal relationship.

Marketing is just as necessary in these areas and may well demand a greater amount of technical expertise. Some organisations are involved in selling both industrial and consumer products, for example companies selling vehicle navigation systems through retailers to vehicle owners and to manufacturers for installation in vehicles.

Business-to-business products

There is a substantial overlap between industrial products and business-to-business (B2B) marketing. B2B is a fairly recent term to describe products bought by offices and factories and by sub-groups such as what has become known as the SOHO market (small office: home office). The range includes all the products an organisation must buy to run its business, such as product components and telephones (and telephone systems), office furniture, paperclips, computer disks and stationery.

In B2B markets brands can be as important as in consumer markets; indeed, some brand names are directed at both. For example, a Mercedes car may be seen as an attractive prestige product, but the name is equally well used for vans and trucks.

Intangible products

Not all products are products. Some are services, and throughout this book "product" should usually be taken to mean product or service. These may be sold to the consumer sector, such as dry cleaning, tax-free savings accounts and film processing; or to other businesses, such as industrial design, contract office cleaning and staff training; or to both, such as accountancy, insurance and hotels.

What characterises services marketing? Services:

▶ are intangible – the fact that they cannot be tested by potential customers before they buy dictates a different approach to marketing and selling;

▶ are inextricably bound up with service – they are the "people businesses", and marketing and the organisation of delivery of the service overlap;

▶ interact directly with customers – much more closely than in some other businesses;

▶ allow change and flexibility to be greater, and sometimes easier and faster, than in other kinds of business (producing a new insurance policy, say, is inherently easier than producing a new jet fighter).

The immediacy of services, in customer service for instance, must be reflected in the way their marketing is organised.

Social marketing

This term is used to describe the marketing activity of not-for-profit organisations such as charities and government bodies which often use specialist marketing service providers to help them. The areas described below all need marketing and provide significant and interesting career opportunities for marketing people.

Charities

Many charities are, by any definition, big businesses. Their target market is contacted to produce funds, and marketing methods may be used in different ways (to change public or government attitudes, for instance). However, marketing is important for them and they need marketing talent to achieve their aims and fulfil their charitable purposes.

Government and other organisations

Both local and national governments have marketing operations. These may be on a grand scale, as with national advertising undertaken to highlight, for example, the dangers of drinking and driving. Or they may draw attention to local schemes to help small businesses.

Other organisations include government agencies, trade bodies (for example, the UK's Wool Marketing Board), educational establishments and professional bodies (such as the Association of Training & Development – ASTD – in the United States). There are many such organisations, some, such as the WWF (World Wide Fund for Nature), with a global remit.

Marketing services

A plethora of specialist services exist within marketing itself to serve commercial and not-for-profit organisations alike. These include advertising agencies, which create advertising for their clients and are specialists in selecting appropriate media, and other more specialised bodies such as agencies to produce point-of-sale promotions, or market research agencies that conduct surveys to identify markets, test products and try to reduce the risk inherent in the marketing process. Even more specialist agencies include those concerned with packaging design, photography or copy writing. As well as working as a part of the marketing process, all such agencies have to market their own services too, and so need to deploy specialist skills on that task.

Industry specialisation

All industries differ to some extent. Some, such as high technology and information technology, professional services, pharmaceuticals and financial services, are highly specialised (not so much technically, but in ways that affect their marketing and the people who undertake it). Furthermore, because the industry is not the only differentiating feature, the size of an organisation and the resources it can therefore employ also affect how marketing is carried out. A small business employing only a handful of people cannot operate like a multinational.

Products in the marketplace

Even when the product is tangible and easily defined, other things affect the precise form that its marketing takes. Market is a broad description. Focusing on a market segment or a niche market (see Chapter 2) helps to make marketing decisions easier – instead of being directed broadly, marketing can concentrate on a particular sector and tailor its approach to it. For example, a pharmaceutical product may aim to appeal only to farmers raising beef cattle and the vets they use; equally, a specialist oil may be suitable for use only in a narrow range of machines.

A product will succeed only if it is good. It must perform, and perform against competition. It does not have to be the best of its sort, but it does need to provide value for money and meet the needs of a sufficient number of customers to pay its way. Some low-cost products are successful. The Bic throw-away ballpoint is not in the same league as a Mont Blanc pen, but it sells in millions and most customers are satisfied that they get value for money. Other organisations such as Bang & Olufsen trade on high quality (and often high price), largely through design. Others market standard and high-specification products separately, as does Toyota with its upmarket Lexus brand of cars.

A good product is essential to marketing success. It is sometimes said that marketing is selling products that do not come back to customers who do.

Making a product unique

A product being good is not enough on its own; it must be good compared with its competitors. Marketers use the term unique selling proposition (USP) to describe whatever it is about a product that differentiates it from others and makes it appeal to customers. The term value proposition is also used in this context.

There is a difference between being the "best" and having a USP that is effective. Best implies superior to, and thus perhaps more expensive than, other products; it implies things being put in rank order. The USP, however, gives a product an edge in its chosen market or market segment, so a simple, less expensive product must appeal to its target market just as much as a sophisticated one. Somewhat like evolution, marketing is part of the constant search for new elements that will keep a product ahead. Unlike evolution, which proceeds by chance with no preconceived aim, marketing intends to succeed at this process. Everything that occurs presents an opportunity. For example, global warming is affecting customer perceptions about many products, but Persil's detergent is advertised as helping to save the planet.

The USP applies just as much to image and communications such as advertising as it does to tangible aspects of the product. It is usually a mix of disparate factors that contribute to a product's success rather than one overriding factor.

The augmented product

What is described as the core product is not enough in itself to guarantee marketing success. It must be added to, to create what is called the augmented product that allows marketers to make more of it.

This involves three layers, and the more a product competes with others the more the outer layers must be worked on:

▶ The core layer is the product itself, with its price inherently tied up with it.

▶ Layer two adds elements to the product to make it more appealing. This might include packaging, a brand name, a level of quality, design or style features, and all the things the product does or means (the benefits, of which more later) to actual and potential customers.

▶ Layer three adds elements that are less inherently part of the product itself. They include a warranty (a comparatively long period is a powerful marketing tool), delivery (and perhaps installation), training in use, after-sales service and financing.

Some things simply add to a product's appeal in the way that an attractive shampoo container can, in part, influence which brand is chosen. They can also become a significant part of the product package – for example, purchasing loan and leasing arrangements are almost as important as the car in that market. They influence both what is bought and where it is bought (different distributors offering identical cars may have very different financing packages).

This helps to explain just how important the product is as a marketing variable – one of the three Ps of the marketing mix (product, price and presentation). The product is in no sense fixed; many decisions have to be made and many tasks undertaken to create a product package that is likely to thrive in a competitive market. Product development (research and development in some contexts) is a continuous process.

This work is always undertaken in a dynamic environment. Things change: when one competitor amends its product package to help differentiate it from competition, the competitor must react and change to stay ahead. Minor differences between products can be significant. For example, one customer may not like the smell of a brand of soap, leaving a choice of many others but with not much to choose between them. Price is important, of course, but the same is no doubt true of brands selling at a similar price. So customers look for some detail that prompts them to buy one brand rather than another. This could be image or a special offer, but it might be a minor product detail. For example, some people like Pears soap partly because its transparency seems to indicate purity.

Positioning the product

Another rule of marketing is that all products need to be positioned with precision within the spectrum of other broadly similar competitive products to make clear what they and their attractions are.

The range of cars, for example, includes city runabouts, family saloons, luxury saloons, sports cars and sports utility vehicles. When introducing a model a manufacturer must be clear how it will be positioned in a way that involves product, image and price. Will the quality, design and price of the car put it at the "top" of the market, or is it to be aimed at people wanting only a basic means of transport at an economy price? Some organisations do both: selling different products under the same brand name at different prices and quality levels. Examples are Perrier Water and Perrier Palace and the different ranges of foods offered by supermarkets under their own brand, such as Wal-Mart's Sam's choice and Great value brands and Tesco's Finest and Value brands. This practice is called premiumisation.

Key points

Marketing approaches are many and varied. Marketing is concerned as much as anything with deciding which of many possible things that might be done will be done and how they will be fitted together (the promotional mix). What is likely to suit, and work best, is primarily influenced by:

▶ the product or service;

▶ the customers towards whom it is directed.

All marketing activity must reflect the nature of the world in which it operates. What is right for marketing chocolate may be very different from what is needed to market ball bearings.

What is crucial in marketing is that:

▶ what is to be marketed is well chosen – a poor product will rarely sell more than once;

▶ marketing activity matches the product in every possible way.

Furthermore, the product and its price are inherently associated.

Pricing policy and tactics

*I am not upset with someone who charges 5
per cent less. I am concerned with someone
who might offer a better experience.*

Jeff Bezos, CEO, Amazon

Setting a product's price is more than picking a "suitable" figure out of the air. It is an important element of marketing and needs serious and systematic consideration, not least of customer attitudes to price. Pricing not only affects profit, it also affects image. The tactical use of price is also very much a part of marketing activity.

How much?

The word that goes most easily with cheap is nasty, yet everyone wants a bargain. But as a bargain is essentially something worth more than it costs (and therefore rare), what they really want is value for money.

A price puts out many messages. It can say something is classy, good quality, fashionable or shoddy. There is an apocryphal story that one of the first astronauts to go to the moon was asked what he thought about in the final few seconds of the countdown. He thought for a moment and said:

> *I remembered that there were 500,000 working parts in the machine underneath me, and that in every case the contract had gone to the lowest bidder.*

Sometimes a low price does not boost customer confidence.

Price has other psychological impacts. For example, much research shows that if a price is just below a round figure, £9.99 or $19.99, rather than £10 or $20, people will buy more. No one really understands why, but many manufacturers and retailers use the fact and set prices accordingly (the other reason is for security – at such prices the shop assistant must give change and thus must open the till and record the sale). The same applies to higher prices, with figures set just below $500, $50,000 and so on.

Similarly, the thinking about discount levels for retailers or wholesalers, quantity terms and so on has to take account of the way people think about the figures. The use of price at annual or seasonal retail sales is another example. Everyone wants to save money, but just how it is put is significant. Which sounds best on a $100 item: "Half price" or "Save $50"? And, if it was reduced to $55, how different do "Almost half price" or "Nearly $50 saved" sound?

Price not only tells customers the cost to be paid, it also indicates quality. Faced with a choice, especially of reasonably technical products such as a camera or a music system, it can be difficult to make a rational decision; price offers a measure – the more expensive one is either better quality or the brand is prestigious. With some products, for instance fashion brands, the high price does not necessarily buy high quality compared with other options, but it buys originality and prestige – people know from the label that a premium price has been paid. Some brands play on this. Bose offers good quality sound systems, but its products are resolutely more highly priced than some of its competitors'. Caterpillar adopts the same strategy for its construction machinery. High price may imply much more, for example long-term service – Canadian outdoor clothes company Tilley offers lifetime guarantees on its famous hats.

Setting pricing policy is a crucial part of a marketer's job, and it is not a once-and-for-all decision – we will charge this much, and put it up by a percentage for inflation each year. Price can be, and is, used tactically, to gain an edge.

Price setting

Many factors must be borne in mind, including the following:

▶ Cost – to make a profit, a product must be sold for more than the cost of making and selling it.

▶ Tax – this is a consideration where tax is added and will affect the price customers see and pay, especially with highly taxed products such as cigarettes and petrol.

▶ Value – this is obvious but also can relate to circumstances. An iced drink on a hot day may command a premium, especially in the only café for miles around.

▶ Market conditions – especially whether demand for a product is increasing or decreasing (something that may happen rapidly or slowly).

▶ Geography – in some places prices of products reflect the cost of isolation (and distribution costs).

▶ Legal restrictions – laws may forbid certain price tactics (such as agreeing prices with competitors).

▶ Consumer preferences – the more desirable something is, the higher the price it can command; an iPhone or at the top end of the scale a Van Gogh painting, for example.

▶ Price sensitivity – some customers are more price sensitive than others. A pensioner on a limited budget, for instance, may forgo buying something if the price rises by even a small amount. A factory may delay replacing machinery for similar reasons.

There are four basic approaches to setting prices based on cost, market demand, competition and the market. These are not mutually exclusive; setting a price should sensibly combine elements of all four approaches.

Cost-based pricing – the accountant's approach

This is an approach that views the situation solely internally (perhaps as an accountant would). It makes assumptions about how the product will be sold and finds a selling price by taking the total cost of the product, including production and marketing plus an allocation of some sort to cover overheads, and a figure for a likely or intended margin.

This approach can help to indicate minimum price levels, but it also has several drawbacks. The cost calculation is based on a pre-determined level of demand and production; as these fluctuate, so does the product's cost. It also ignores market factors such as demand and competitors' actions. In addition, the way overheads are allocated can lead to wrong pricing decisions.

Market demand-based pricing – the economist's approach

The aim of this approach is to explore the effect that different prices may have on demand. The marketer will try to calculate the break-even point (using varying volume forecasts) based on different selling prices in order to find the most profitable price/volume ratio. Marketers must ask themselves how many units of a given product they could sell at different price levels.

The advantage of this approach is that it brings together price calculations with market demand realities; if demand for a product is a function of its price, this should be a determining factor in the decision.

The disadvantage is the difficulty of estimating the effect of price variations on demand; estimates of how many units can be sold at a given price level must be made. An easy way to establish price elasticity is to examine the historical performance of similar products at a number of different price levels.

Competition-based pricing

This method involves considering the prices set by competitors in the marketplace and then deciding whether to set prices above, below or at the same level as competitors' products.

In most markets collusion between competitors to fix prices is illegal. Legislation may also regulate prices in specialist areas such as public transport fares. In London, for instance, competing bus companies are required to charge the same fares.

Market-based pricing

This method bases price on the perceived value the product delivers to the buyer, which can be a result of:

▶ value for money influenced by all aspects of an organisation and its product or service;

▶ image affected by status (endorsement by opinion leaders, exclusivity or promotion);

▶ reflection of different and distinctive market segments putting different values on a product's performance;

▶ price barriers apparent in different segments.

It is crucial to assess accurately the market's perception of the product's value. Market research may be needed to avoid two dangers:

▶ overpricing because of an inflated view of the value of a product – almost inevitably the perceived price will be a qualitative judgment made by the buyer relative to experience of the competition;

▶ underestimating the real value and charging less than is possible, thus reducing the profit earned.

There can be many, sometimes conflicting, things to bear in mind. Thus price setting is often a compromise.

Pricing strategies

Given a price range in a particular area of the market, a decision has to be made as to where in that range to locate a product's price. This is a strategic decision made according to an organisation's objectives, which may include the need to:

▶ achieve a target return on investment or sales;

▶ maintain or improve market share;

▶ meet or prevent competition.

Some tactical approaches to price are described below.

Skim pricing

This is where a price is set at the top of the acceptable range. It is used:

▶ on a new product in the early stages of its life-cycle to recoup high investment;

▶ to segment the market;

▶ to prevent pricing mistakes by setting the price too low – it is easier to reduce prices than to increase them if the wrong price level is chosen initially;

▶ to limit demand if planned capacity or stocks are not adequate.

Its disadvantages are that:

▶ it may encourage competition;

▶ the lower volume sales it results in may not suit production objectives;

▶ it may hinder consumer awareness and acceptance in the introductory life stage for a new product;

▶ it makes the product more vulnerable to less advantageous economic conditions.

A good example of skim pricing being used to good effect is with technology products such as mobile phones. Typically a new model with new features has an initially high price, but this drops as further new models come into the market at high prices in their turn. The cycle is apparent to all and some customers just wait until the price falls before buying.

Penetration pricing

This is the opposite of skimming. A low price is set, often below the existing range of the competition, with the aim of gaining maximum market penetration as quickly as possible; that is, low price, high volume.

Among its advantages are that:

▶ it permits a lower product cost as a result of large-scale production;

▶ it helps to pre-empt competition;

▶ it makes the winning of wide product allegiance for the future more likely.

Among its disadvantages are that:

▶ the profit per unit is lower and usually the pay-back period is longer for a new product;

▶ it is unlikely to have the desired effect if the product has a short life-cycle;

▶ it can be difficult to overcome the psychological disadvantages of having to increase the price if it was set too low initially.

Marginal cost pricing

In highly competitive situations there may be an opportunity to gain business if a sufficiently low price is offered. This raises the question: what is the lowest price at which it makes sense to take the business? One approach is to use marginal costing – calculating the cost of producing one extra unit. The existing sales volume covers the fixed costs and the costs of producing the extra unit are variables. If a small profit is made per unit, it is an additional contribution that would not have been made if the extra business had not been gained. Even at no profit, marginal business may be worth having as it may use resources that would otherwise stand idle – for example, a hotel room – and potentially generate profit in another part of the business, such as the restaurant or business centre.

Marginal cost pricing, however, can ultimately eat into profits and depress the percentage return on sales. It can also drive down the normal price as word gets around that the organisation engages in it. The main use of marginal costing, therefore, is to answer the question "should I accept this order?" rather than as a pricing tool. Marginal cost pricing is more often used with price-elastic, high-volume products, where it is important to keep the sales volume up. So it is common with exports: to be competitive in foreign markets, elements of cost already covered by home sales are ignored in setting the overseas prices.

Pricing in context

With all such considerations marketers must bear in mind that pricing is not seen by the purchaser simply in terms of what is cheapest, but rather as one element in the bundle of benefits – what the image of the product is in the mind of the consumer/user and hence the perceived value. Customers never buy on price alone. Note that few successful operators, and few brand leaders, are at the low price end of their markets, though some do this intentionally and successfully – furniture and household goods retailer IKEA and airlines such as Ryanair and Southwest are examples. Yet many sales people often argue that price is the sole purchasing motivator. So before marketers comment on competitive pricing strategies or price structure, they must make sure they know the relevant facts or they may well make pricing recommendations that are unnecessary or wrong.

Day-to-day tactics

Many price-setting techniques are used to boost sales and profits (perhaps only temporarily), including the following:

▶ Prestige pricing – setting a high price to encourage a feeling of exclusivity, in the way that caviar, inexpensive in local markets, is priced up when exported.

▶ Variable pricing – charging different prices at different times (for example, trains and cinemas) or for different people (such as reduced fares for children or special rates for senior citizens).

▶ Geography and type of store – for example, in London Tesco Express will charge higher prices in Hampstead than in Clapham Junction.

▶ Set prices – everything under $10.

▶ Bundling – setting a price for a "package"; for instance, a computer with a particular suite of software (Microsoft has thrived on this) or a holiday with car hire included;

▶ Trade-in allowances – as with trading in a car or upgrading industrial equipment.

▶ Quantity discount – a host of pricing devices link buying greater quantities to a lower unit cost.

▶ Seasonal variations – in retail this is often linked to seasonal sales or newly introduced products at a higher price.

▶ Timing – a price for today or this month only.

▶ Price plus extras – a basic price is made to look good value, but other items need to be added on (for instance, a digital camera almost never has any significant memory, which has to be bought as an extra).

Pricing may also be affected by other elements of the product and purchase mix, as with the financial arrangements (loan or leasing) for buying a car.

Marketers often overreact when facing competitive price pressure. Not only are brand leaders rarely the cheapest; they are also frequently among the most expensive. It is more likely that setting prices too low will do more damage rather than the reverse. If prices and margins are high, more can be spent on marketing – and probably needs to be – to generate the desired sales volume.

Pricing is an important – and creative – aspect of the marketing job. A marketing plan should include actual prices, costs and margins at various levels (the pricing structure). Prices of major competitive products should also be considered along with the price structure for different buyers: wholesalers or whatever. A brief statement of the pricing strategy and of the various pricing considerations must also feature in the plan summarising the options and decisions. A systematic approach to setting price is summarised below.

Creating image through price

With most products price and image are inextricably linked. This is important because it has a direct bearing on how successful a product will be and how much profit it will generate.

Do customers want the cheapest product? Yes, but not if low price means inadequacies. What customers really want is value for money. They are prepared to pay more for products of superior

Six steps to price setting

An organisation must:

▶ carefully establish its marketing objective(s), such as survival, current profit maximisation, market share leadership or product quality leadership;

▶ determine the demand schedule, which shows the probable quantity purchased per period at alternative price levels – the more inelastic the demand, the higher the company can set its price;

▶ estimate how its costs vary at different output levels and with different levels of accumulated production experience;

▶ examine competitors' prices as a basis for positioning its own price;

▶ utilise as appropriate cost-plus pricing, break-even analysis and a target-profit pricing, perceived-value pricing, going-rate pricing or tender pricing;

▶ select its final price, expressing it in the most effective psychological way, checking that it conforms with company pricing policies and making sure it will prevail with distributors and dealers, the company's sales force, competitors, suppliers and government.

Tactical fine-tuning must then continue over time.

quality. Rolls-Royce and the word cheap do not go together. The consumer expects a Rolls-Royce to command a Rolls-Royce price, so much so that other products become known as "The Rolls-Royce of X" (despite Rolls-Royce's vigilance in protecting the trademark) and are priced accordingly. Many producers visibly use this in their offering. For example, Stella Artois, a Belgian beer, was sold for many years as "Reassuringly expensive".

How is the right price decided upon? It must be one that a sufficient number of customers will pay taking into account the market segment and the level of competition. Thus there is a framework for deciding if there is a gap in the market that can be filled profitably.

Another approach that has become common is confusion pricing of such things as mobile phone tariffs. The prices are so complex that easy comparison with the competition is difficult or impossible and consumer choice is effectively limited. This may work for a while, but there is always the danger of a consumer backlash or a competitor setting itself apart from what is happening in an industry and achieving positive differentiation.

Many techniques are designed to get a better impact from the marketing power of pricing. Two for the price of one is an everyday example. Sometimes called BOGOF (buy one, get one free), it may be offered to shift stock or as part of a plan linked to promotion.

Price and human psychology

Price is important, but it is not the only consideration of the sale, so how can the price be maximised without losing sales? Change is the norm in dynamic markets and marketers must constantly strive to set the "best" price. For example, after having done all the research, a product may be launched at a price so compelling that it is difficult for production to keep up with demand. This raises the question: should the price be raised to dampen down the market and maximise profit or will this damage the consumer's expectation of the new product and encourage competitors to undercut the price? Pricing decisions are often complex and getting them wrong can damage brand image (especially for products at the top end of the market) and cause a price war that may be difficult to stop. There is no one as fickle as a customer.

Pricing is an area in which sophisticated modelling can be used but judgment remains crucial. Common mistakes made in pricing strategy include:

▶ pricing decisions being too biased towards cost structures rather than market considerations;

▶ prices being set independently of other elements of the marketing mix;

▶ taking too little account of opportunities to capitalise on differentiation;

▶ prices not varying greatly between different market segments;

▶ pricing policy being defensive – led by events rather than being one of the prime marketing tools.

Analysing the product and the market is a prerequisite to making effective pricing decisions. This means asking:

▶ How large is the product market in terms of buying potential? A thorough understanding and evaluation of the potential market is needed before considering the pricing of the product.

▶ What segments exist in the product market and what market target strategy is to be used? Different market segments seek different benefits and expect to pay different prices. Clearly identifying the segments and their profile is crucial in price setting.

▶ How sensitive is demand in any segment to change in price? This relates to price elasticity – the principle that if price is dropped, a larger quantity of something will be sold, whereas if price is increased, the volume of sales may drop. If the percentage change in quantity is more than the percentage change in price, the product is price elastic; if it is less, the product is price inelastic. It is easy to get this wrong and misjudge the acceptable price range. Prices set outside the potential buyers' acceptable range mean lost sales.

▶ How important are non-price issues such as features and locations? Products must be differentiated and it may be better to enhance the product or service features as a competitive tool rather than to vary price.

▶ What are the estimated sales at different price levels? Levels of promotion will also affect sales, so this and other factors must be taken into account when setting prices.

Key points

▶ The price is an inherent part of any product and used by customers to make judgments and decisions.

▶ Setting the price must be considered broadly, not just in the context of a short-term calculation of costs.

▶ The price is rarely fixed for long and can be used tactically and creatively as an inherent part of the overall marketing approach.

▶ A systematic approach to making pricing decisions and policy may work best, but there is no guaranteed formula for getting it "right".

Market research: reducing the risk

I don't think anyone ought to be making marketing decisions without some form of research because you can waste a lot of time and money.

Herbert Baum, CEO, Hasbro

Sound information can provide a firm basis for effective marketing activity. The various techniques of market research can provide pertinent, objective information, helping an organisation to operate without undue risk. Marketing must try to accurately meet customer needs and respond to a variety of circumstances in every aspect of the environment in which it operates. Some information that will help is well known, but some is less obvious and there is a danger of making assumptions without establishing the facts.

Marketing and uncertainty

The net effect of the dynamic environment in which marketing operates can be summed up in one word: risk. Business is an uncertain undertaking. For example, if you launch a new product (reputedly with a success rate of only one in ten), the risk is all too obvious. In some businesses, for instance manufacturing a new aircraft, the long lead times and massive capital requirements make the risk huge. It is management's job to assess risk when making decisions, and good decision-making is helped by information and knowledge. This is where market research – a body of techniques that provides information to assist management decision-making – comes in.

It does not remove judgment and experience from the process; rather it supports them by providing a better basis of fact. It can do a wide range of things from confirming a suspicion to unearthing new, previously unthought-of facts. Sometimes this new information changes matters just a little and sometimes more significantly, as when Johnson & Johnson discovered that it could sell more Band-Aids by putting characters from children's stories on them. Equally, not researching a market can be costly, as in the case of an American company that set up a factory in the UK to manufacture weatherproofing for flat roofs, only to discover too late that flat roofs are far less common in the UK than the United States.

Market research is undertaken in order to add to the objective element of decision-making, to make it better informed and ultimately more likely to take business in the right direction. In all its forms, market research has one overriding purpose: to reduce risk and thus increase the likelihood of success.

Market research – why bother?

Sometimes people believe in "knowing your market" and that research is an expensive luxury; there are some success stories involving no research of any sort, though the fact that the most quoted is the Sony Walkman, launched on a hunch of the chairman, seems to indicate that this is not common. In general, to make good decisions you need good information. The information of most concern to marketing management comes from research into markets and customers, present, potential and future, and concerns the shape, size, nature, needs, opportunities and threats within the market.

Market research can be defined as:

> The systematic problem analysis, model-building and fact-finding for the purpose of improved decision-making and control in the marketing of goods and services.

This implies that market research provides not just information, but also guidance to help improve the abilities of management and a means of making a contribution to managing the marketing mix. It can be used, for example, to help decide the marketing strategy required to exploit new opportunities, which gaps in the market should be investigated and where the most potential lies.

Two important uses of research are to:

▶ reduce uncertainty when plans are being made, whether these relate to the marketing operation as a whole or to individual components of the marketing mix such as advertising or sales promotion;

▶ monitor performance after the plans have been put into operation. This role itself has two specific functions: to help to control the execution of the company's operational plan and to make a substantial contribution to long-term strategic planning.

Simply stated, research covers all the "finding out" activities of marketing. The methods used may be simple, such as a questionnaire placed in a hotel bedroom. Collecting and analysing the responses indicates the views of guests on subjects such as the shortcomings of the accommodation or the efficiency of the online booking system. Thus some research can be simply done without vast cost.

Other methods may be complicated, with data being gathered by mail, telephone or e-mail; through face-to-face interviews with large numbers of people spread widely, maybe internationally; or through focus groups, where people are asked for their views on a product or service.

Research is undertaken in the early stages of a marketing process to identify consumers' needs and in later stages to track changes. For example, a research project conducted by the UK's telecommunications group BT brought immediate results. Sue Burdon, head of brand and communications research at TNS UK, which conducted the study, says:

> BT's consumer advertising tracking research ... is designed to show the effect of the communications on the brand, and to advise on ways to improve communications effectiveness and efficiency. Based on our findings in the first year, we were able to show BT that they could make changes to their brand communications programme to use fewer ads and modify the spend patterns.

BT took these findings on board and was able to increase the impact of its campaign while also making substantial savings. This programme won Best Advertising Research at *Marketing* magazine's Market Research awards in 2008.

Market research is an umbrella term for different types of research including specific research into markets (see Table 5.1).

Table 5.1 Five kinds of market research

Market research	As an individual technique, this investigates markets, asking who buys what and in what quantity
Product research	Focuses on the product or service, asking what is right and wrong with the product or service or some aspect of it
Marketing method research	Examines aspects of marketing activity to see how well it is operating, asking whether communication, distribution and so on are effective
Motivational research	Looks at the way people think, asking why they buy the products they do and what they feel about them
Attitude survey	Focuses on customers' perceptions of and attitudes to products and the companies that make them

Like any other form of research, market research – in the sense of all the different kinds of research – can only investigate past and present behaviour, attitudes and motivations. It is not possible to research the future.

However, research helps to predict future behaviour, such as voting intentions. But predictions based on opinion polls or about likely future purchasing decisions are far from infallible. One researcher (quoted anonymously at a Market Research Society conference) said:

> *Good research reveals things I didn't know. Indifferent research reveals things I already knew. Bad research concentrates on things I know are untrue.*

The role of research, therefore, is to improve the facts on which forecasts and decisions are made. It must focus on information that is helpful and on making sure that information is as accurate as possible.

The role of market research

Market research provides information that helps an organisation to define opportunities for product development and market strategy. It works by assessing whether marketing strategies are accurately targeted and by identifying market opportunities or changes that customers need. Market research can (usefully) confirm issues that are well known in a market initially, and if planned and executed well, it will identify new opportunities, market niches or ways to improve sales, marketing and communications activities. Even quite simple matters can be significant in effect. For instance, research at a major confectionery company showed that a new spherical-shaped chocolate, which was about to be dropped because of problems in producing the desired shape, would have greater appeal as an irregular shape. This saved the company from wasting a £250,000 investment and led to a successful launch.

Five specific uses of market research are:

▶ to define the size, shape and nature of a market so as to identify the marketing opportunities;

▶ to investigate the strengths and weaknesses of competitive products and the level of trade support a company enjoys;

▶ to test ideas about products and marketing strategy in order to help define the most effective customer-led strategies;

▶ to monitor the effectiveness of marketing strategies;

▶ to help determine when marketing expenditure, promotions and targeting need to be adjusted or improved.

Market research is not simply a "first check". It is useful ahead of any action, and also provides a means of checking and refining views as operations proceed. The best results come when marketing and sales planning is influenced by the results of research; in other words, when research pays for itself by providing a basis for change and improving operations.

Other reasons for undertaking market research include the following:

▶ to provide data on the market, or a market segment, and to discover whether the sector is increasing, staying the same or decreasing in importance to customers;

▶ to obtain information to help understand who the customers are and the way in which they buy and use certain products;

▶ to assess what customers feel about the services they are receiving and their quality;

▶ to research customer attitudes and needs on a continuous basis to find out which product types are selling and where there are opportunities for new sales;

▶ to achieve better targeting by identifying which consumers are likely to buy the product and understanding what media and messages will influence their decision;

▶ to identify changes in the market that will affect the marketing approach in future.

Market research is central to the marketing process, underpinning the actions taken and helping to clarify what should be focused on. To summarise, market research:

▶ is a means to an end and can help to improve marketing effectiveness and reduce business risk;

▶ encompasses a range of different kinds of research that can be deployed to help in a variety of ways;

▶ is not infallible, despite using "scientific" methods such as statistical techniques; it provides guidance that informs and supports the management judgment that is always needed;

▶ although fallible, is a valuable marketing tool.

Market research techniques

There are many techniques and methodologies in market research. Using them demands specialist skills and adaptability because the techniques themselves are constantly developing and changing. Using them successfully depends on experience of both market research and the broader issues of marketing.

In this section a number of factors are outlined briefly under a series of headings that illustrate the market research process and highlight important issues. They are arranged broadly chronologically, starting with preparing for research. Further study will identify additional specialist approaches, such as research into advertising methods, radio listening and more.

Planning market research surveys

Lurking behind most research surveys is a problem that needs solving – including a "positive problem" such as seeking to find the best way to exploit an opportunity. At the outset the researcher must define the problem and show how it may be solved. The researcher must develop skills in taking a brief from the "problem owner" and translating it into a "proposal" for carrying out the study. In the proposal the researcher states the objectives of the study, the methods that will be used to meet the objectives, the timing, the composition of the research team and the cost. This is the case whether an organisation is undertaking research itself or using a specialist agency.

Desk research

There is no point in "reinventing the wheel", which is costly and time consuming. If up-to-date data exist, they should be used and not reinvestigated. Desk research is the collection, sifting and interpretation of published data. It plays a part in most surveys, even if only to use the known breakdown of the population to guide the selection of a quota sample. Elsewhere it may involve the researcher using the library or searching online databases for information on market size and structure. This is an area where information technology has created many new options.

Standards and methods

Standards have increasingly affected the practice of market research. In the UK these relate primarily to the Market Research Society's Code of Conduct, which seeks to reassure the general public that research is carried out in a professional and ethical manner and is used appropriately. For example, the MRS seeks to prevent research being used to disguise a sales pitch. Such attitudes are common in the industry. The American Marketing Research Association regards maintaining the ethics of the business as one of its most important roles.

Standards do not define good methods, but they encourage attention to quality. They are intended to be implemented at an organisational level, rather than being a matter for individual researchers – but they must be followed by researchers in an organisation and are there to promote consumer confidence in the process. Without consumers' co-operation, no research is possible.

Sampling and statistics

Researchers must get sampling right. The mathematical basis that allows small numbers to be researched with the confidence that they are truly representative of the population as a whole (whatever the group is) is crucial. Understanding the rudiments of random sampling is essential, even though in most day-to-day surveys the researcher may learn to trust a quota sample of, say, 300 interviews spread across five cities. Without appreciating why and how different samples are selected, the researcher cannot claim to be undertaking a valid, scientific piece of work. Research must therefore be based on specialist knowledge about sampling.

Questionnaire design

Good market research involves asking the right people the right questions – and those questions must be clear and unambiguous. In theory, questionnaire design should be easy, yet it is one of the most difficult things to get right. Researchers must strive to ask questions that draw out accurate information, can be answered easily by the interviewee, flow well and leave respondents feeling that they have made a worthwhile contribution. This is an important part of any study.

Geodemographics

Survey samples used to be selected from a representative quota of the population based on sex, social class and age. Over the past 20 years, however, it has become possible to link the characteristics of people with the neighbourhoods in which they live. This allows researchers to infer certain types of behaviour in different localities and is important when research is directed widely across the population as a whole. For a company wanting to research buyers of, say, agricultural machinery, identifying the people to contact is less of a problem.

Quantitative research

Quantitative research supplies a number for anything that can be measured; indeed, many researchers argue that anything can be measured. Quantitative research produces "hard" data that can be defended or challenged and is more than just opinion. It is based on sizeable surveys using samples of 200 people or more. However, it is often appropriate to plumb people's opinions, first using qualitative techniques (see page 64) before determining exactly what should be measured. The qualitative and quantitative methods are often used together in this way, although it is always easier to give findings credence when something measurable is involved.

Quantitative research over the internet

The internet has become a collection of virtual communities, all focused on sharing information. For some organisations the internet may be no more than a marketing or promotional tool, but others benefit from providing their services via the internet. It provides a new method of collecting and distributing information, making web and e-mail questionnaires useful for market researchers. Market research using the internet is constantly changing and becoming more sophisticated, as are associated applications.

Face-to-face interviewing

The market research industry has been built around face-to-face interviewing – in the street and in the home – and research in the office. Such interviews remain the bedrock of many studies as they allow the interviewer to use personal skills to elicit the information in a way that enhances accuracy. Such personal contact also allows visual aids to be used (as does the internet), smooths the interview and allows deeper insights to be gained than do more mechanistic methods. But much depends on the skill of the interviewer.

Telephone interviewing

Telephone interviewing became popular as a market research tool in the 1980s. Interviews can be carried out speedily and controlled closely. The researcher can easily sample households anywhere, either at home or abroad. It is not necessarily cheap; costs are similar to those of street interviews. Again, much depends on the skill of the interviewer in making sure the responses are genuine.

Postal surveys

Sending a questionnaire by mail is one of the simplest methods of conducting a survey, but some people believe these surveys generate inadequate responses, usually because they are used in the wrong circumstances. They produce excellent results when there is a strong relationship between the respondent and the company carrying out the research. They are suited to testing opinion on sensitive subjects and work best with closed questions. Different styles and approaches are designed to maximise responses.

Research by mail needs careful thought if it is to generate useful results. For example, just changing a heading or adding further explanatory text can make a difference. So can using incentives, such as offering a reward to respondents who complete questionnaires; the reward might be some kind of gift or the chance to win a large sum in a prize draw.

Omnibus research

Omnibus studies target certain groups and are run at regular intervals. They allow an organisation to buy space for a specified number of questions in a large interview programme. This is a cost-efficient way to collect data because the cost of interviewing and analysis is shared among several organisations. An ever-expanding range of omnibus surveys covering all manner of target groups has sprung up over the years.

Panels and diaries

A panel differs from an omnibus study because it surveys the same people each time. In practice, it is not always exactly the same people all the time as some drop out. Care is taken to replace departing panel members with others with similar demographic characteristics. The questions asked are consistent so that results can be tracked over time to provide reliable trend data on purchasing or on such matters as television viewing habits. Panels are usually sponsored by large media groups or companies wanting to monitor movements in their target markets. The panel members record their purchases and activities in special diaries.

Retail audits

Retail audits take place in shops. By monitoring inventory turnover, such audits produce accurate figures on the market shares of a wide range of consumer goods. For example, Nielsen Book-Scan tracks the book sales of major booksellers. Subscribers use the audit results to monitor changes in brand shares and within the distribution routes through which their goods are sold. This allows them to adjust their strategies in the marketplace to meet changing conditions.

EPOS

Electronic point of sale (EPOS) is the process of scanning bar codes at the checkout, typically, though not only, at retail outlets. This allows researchers to measure quickly and accurately which goods have been sold and at what prices. This is an excellent means of tracking sales data of different products as well as providing a basis for much predictive modelling. Loyalty cards also track who is buying what, where and how often.

Qualitative research

Researchers often need to understand not just what is happening, but why and how something is happening. To achieve this, the qualitative researcher works with small samples of people, sometimes on a one-to-one basis and sometimes in small groups. The process is more like a conversation or discussion than an interview. The sessions can be long and unstructured and considerable skill is required to draw out relevant information, and even more to analyse the significant facts from them afterwards. Qualitative research can produce rich data, probing into people's unconscious attitudes and needs. The samples are small so there is no attempt to measure responses. To recap, quantitative research is concerned with numbers (40% of voters are likely to vote for a particular political party), whereas qualitative research might show that what influences voters most is, say, the level of tax they are likely to have to pay under a particular government.

In-depth interviews

Using open-ended and unstructured interview guides, the researcher uses this technique to "get beneath" the superficial responses. The in-depth interview allows the researcher to be flexible in the order and style of questioning so that avenues of interest and relevance to a particular respondent can be explored. This can be a valuable technique, but it can be expensive.

Group discussions (focus groups)

A group discussion, which usually involves between five and ten people, involves an exchange of views and is led by the researcher (the moderator). The interactions between people in the group are used to flush out views that would not otherwise be raised in one-to-one interviewing. This technique is used widely for researching new concepts and guiding creative decision-making. Group sessions can yield rich information, but they must be directed by experienced researchers to make them work and to obtain true responses, not just the "party line". Here, too, costs can be high.

Hall tests

There are many occasions when it is necessary for people to look at (or touch or taste) a product, but for all sorts of reasons it may not be possible to do this in consumers' homes. In this case, hall tests are set up. Target consumers are "recruited" on the street and invited to a nearby venue ("hall") where the test takes place. A variety of techniques may be used, but all use the product itself as part of the inquiry.

Sensory evaluation

This tool helps technical research and development teams to design better products. It focuses on just a few important aspects of a product such as the materials used to make it, their quality, the shape of the product and its performance in use. Data can be mapped to show where the product stands against consumer preferences and in comparison with the competition. Because the evaluation considers a number of variables, this type of new product research benefits greatly from multivariate analysis.

Making use of the data

A "pile of data", no matter how carefully assembled, is of little value in its own right. It needs interpreting to be useful in decision-making.

Collecting the data

There are many methods for pulling together the raw data. They are not mutually exclusive and a mixture may be used in many research projects. Some methods match logically with a particular target audience, which may be so numerous that only low-cost methods are possible, or so difficult to contact that special – and more expensive – methods are the only way.

Data analysis

Data have no value in isolation. It is the implications of data that really matter – what is shown or suggested. This means that researchers must tease out only the data relevant to the study's objectives and simplify them so that the user can quickly and easily see a pattern. The data must be presented in a form that can be understood and, it is hoped, lead naturally to conclusions and recommendations. This part of the process may be conducted largely by computer, but the job of setting up the required analysis is an important and skilled one.

Modelling

Computer modelling allows researchers to get more out of their data than ever before. For example, programs exist for testing the prices that people will pay for a product. They can show the degree to which consumers will trade off feature such as quality or design against price. Simulated test markets can be set up. Missing data can be inferred by combining different sets of data. Data can be analysed to map or segment consumers according to their characteristics or attitudes to brands. The results are helpful in determining what action to take. Such modelling is complex and may be beyond the resources of many small organisations, but technological change is making it more accessible to them.

Despite the sophistication and variety of techniques involved in modelling, mistakes still happen. For example, in a test of Knorr soups in the United States, potential consumers in a taste test were positive about them, but the subsequent launch was disappointing. It transpired that people were prejudiced against the powdered form of soups – but no questions had been asked about that.

Presentations and reports

Presentations are the "day of reckoning" for researchers, a chance to make a mark for better or worse. Good presentations have a clear objective. They are short but to the point with little time spent describing the method and more time spent on the findings and conclusions. The use of charts and diagrams to communicate the data has become increasingly sophisticated, and software programs such as PowerPoint make it easy to produce clear information quickly and cheaply, though not necessarily effectively.

While a personal presentation has an impact, a written report is more enduring and may be read over a long period of time. The same rules apply as to presentations. The audience must be kept in mind and the writing style should communicate the points quickly and clearly, leading logically to the conclusions and recommendations. Most people cannot grasp complex figures and their implications instantly; and most find charts helpful in understanding the meaning of the figures.

Research as a generator of success

The risks faced by businesses today have never been greater. Competition is fierce at every level of every market. The cost of failure can be high for both entrepreneurs and established large businesses.

Success and failure in business are a consequence of making the right or wrong decisions. The right decisions are easy with hindsight, but much more difficult when the conditions are unknown. It is relatively simple to plan the production resources and estimate the financial requirement for a business, yet both must be based on understanding the needs of the market and on whether customers will buy the products and then become repeat buyers.

It is a proper understanding of the market that is most often misjudged; assumptions are often made or things are taken for granted. Uncertainty about what the market wants, both now and in the future, is one of the great difficulties with which businesses must cope. More than ever, decisions in business require robust information. If information on markets is important to business success, it follows that the people who can supply it hold considerable power.

The role of market researchers is to provide sound information to guide business decisions. Marketing people and senior management are responsible for making sure that they do, so that they can set strategies and monitor their implementation.

Research pays dividends. For example, over the years, HarperCollins, Agatha Christie's publisher, used gory illustrations (a bloody knife or corpse) on the covers of her crime novels. Then in the early 2000s research showed that people regarded her crimes as "nice" and that the appeal of the books was essentially as mysteries. After redesigning the covers, sales rose by 40% in a year (nearly 500,000 additional books).

The techniques available to researchers have been developed and polished, especially over the past three decades. There is no area in which market research techniques cannot be used. They are as useful in social marketing to probe why people drink and drive as they are to manufacturers selling alcoholic drinks, to the government trying to recruit people for the armed forces, or to theatre managers trying to measure the likes and dislikes of their potential audiences. The skill of the market researcher is not just being able to apply particular techniques, but also knowing which to apply and when.

Although research can only predict the future, some of the trends it highlights can have wide-ranging effects. A study by Envirosell, an American research group, suggests that ageing populations will mean that information on products, packaging and so on should be larger (checking such details is part of how people shop). This seems sensible when you consider the tiny type used in much food content labelling, but will it be heeded?

Key points

Market research is not a panacea able to cure all business ills, but it is useful in an organisation's battle to survive and prosper in the harsh commercial world:

▶ It is complex and specialist, demanding that the right mix of techniques is used in the right way (something that may also demand specialist expertise).

▶ Its findings can assist in the decision-making process, but it does not replace the judgment that is necessary in the interpretation of research findings.

▶ It is only ever as good as its brief – if the wrong questions are asked of the wrong people, the findings will be neither reliable nor useful.

Lack of research, or bad research, can seriously handicap – and at worst cripple – an organisation. For many organisations, it is not just a desirable option but an operational necessity, without which they are effectively operating with one arm tied behind their back

Routes to market: distribution channels and methodology

*Channels exist to serve consumers. Their
purpose is similar to that of brands. Both
exist to build superior customer value very
efficiently for above average profits.*

Hugh Davidson, author of *Even More Offensive Marketing*

An organisation is linked to the world outside by its marketing. There is a huge gulf between a production process and a factory and customers actually buying, using and finding a product satisfactory. Distribution is the umbrella term for everything that links an organisation with the outside world. This chapter focuses on the processes and techniques that set up a route (or routes) to market. Making the right decisions in this area and making the chosen methodology work well are integral to marketing being effective.

The way to market: the need for distribution

Marketing must link to the market, not just in terms of having a focus on customers and their needs, but literally. This link, involving the "place" P of marketing, is provided by distribution.

Marketing people must get to grips with the methodology concerning distribution channels – the network of organisations needed to distribute goods or services from manufacturers to consumers. This network comprises manufacturers, distributors, wholesalers and retailers. Marketers also use the term "chains of distribution" to describe the various kinds of linked intermediaries involved.

However good and well-promoted a product or service is, and however much customers and potential customers want it, it has to be put in a position that gives people easy access to it. It must be distributed. This can be a complex marketing variable, albeit one that is sometimes regarded as rather more fixed than it actually is. Goods are made available in a variety of ways. Consumer products are sold by retailers, which may vary enormously in nature, from supermarkets and department stores, to specialist retailers, general stores and even market traders. They may be located in a town or city centre, in an out-of-town shopping area, in a multi-storey shopping centre or on a neighbourhood corner site – or they may be virtual retailers, selling online or through direct mail catalogues.

The complexity does not stop there. Retailers may buy direct from the producer or be supplied by a network of wholesalers or distributors; some consumer products are sold by mail order, through the internet, by door-to-door salesmen or through home parties (like Tupperware). It is much the same with services; even traditional banking services are available in stores, from machines, through post and telephone, via the internet and even on a drive-in basis. The business-to-business and industrial products sectors are just as varied in the range of options they use to get their products to their customers. Export markets add further complexity.

Similar chains of distribution exist in the marketing of every kind of product. See the section on market maps (page 74) for an example.

New channels of distribution now exist as a result of the IT revolution and the advent of various forms of e-commerce, adding a new dimension to the challenges of channel management – the process of managing the distribution of products and services and the various external organisations and people involved.

Channel management

Efficient distribution is a prerequisite of any product being purchased, at least in any quantity.

Distribution is more than just setting up a mechanism to make goods available. It also acts as part of the process that persuades people to buy. In other words, the quality of distribution – how well the various channels work – is a marketing variable. Managing the distribution process is a crucial part of marketing activity and is conceptually no different from implementing a creative advertising campaign. There are several separate, but linked, aspects to channel management.

Channel choice

Decisions must be made about which channels will be used (and which will not). When channels are not mutually exclusive, several may be used together and the mix (and relative importance of different channels) must be decided. This is not choice as if from a shopping list. Some channels are common and used in a standard form. Alternatively, an organisation's managers may come up with their own way of using that channel, sometimes creating entirely new approaches. Different companies in the same industry may have different approaches. For example, Dell's computers are primarily sold direct; Apple owns its own retail outlets as well as selling through selected retailers; and other manufacturers reach the end customer though specialist computer stores or general retailers.

Directing marketing activity towards different channels

Different channels involve reaching customers in different ways and may need different approaches and techniques. That often makes the sales element important. For example, one channel may contain customers who can be handled successfully by the sales force; another may demand a more sophisticated approach using key account managers.

Managing the channel at unit level

Most distribution channels involve more than one party. It is important to build and maintain constructive relationships with all parties involved and give them what they need to do the best possible job, such as good and timely product information and sales material. It may also require incentives, which are increasingly demanded by retailers in terms of discounts and promotion fees.

How a company analyses the distribution possibilities and selects a method or methods effectively is crucial to overall marketing success. It is also affected by overall trends in the marketplace – for example, the growing importance of out-of-town superstores or online selling.

Success is also in the details, everything from the strategic view of channel management to the practicalities and tactics of working through individual wholesalers or retailers. Because the elements involved in this area of marketing are complex and interlocking, what matters is the overall mix and how it is managed. The main issues for marketers are to:

▶ make good channel choice decisions and never regard them as fixed for ever;

▶ tailor marketing approaches for each channel;

▶ manage the relationships involved, especially where success depends on people along the chain over whom no direct control is possible;

▶ focus on the customer – no scheme and no channel will bring commercial success unless it is satisfactory in consumer terms; ideally, customers must find that it meets their needs and is entirely to their tastes.

The impact of distribution on marketing success

The importance of distribution to marketing – positive or negative – is shown by how it works in practice. For example, someone wanting to buy a piece of equipment may (reasonably) want it demonstrated. If a particular stockist will not do this, the potential customer is likely go elsewhere. Or a customer may need a product by a certain date which one stockist can guarantee but another cannot.

The availability options

Products may be widely available. Mars or Hershey bars, for example, can be bought from supermarkets, local stores, newsagents, filling stations, cinemas, leisure centres, clubs, bars, vending machines, cafes, sandwich shops and so on, all located in a variety of places. By contrast, Wedgwood china is sold through exclusive dealers and might be (intentionally) available in only one shop in a particular town.

Change in availability can prompt rapid customer reaction. Closing down an option may have a disastrous effect on sales but a new option, if convenient, may have the reverse effect. Old habits may die hard, but if a change is attractive and visible, new sales and distribution practices can quickly be established and even become the norm. Note the rapid uptake of internet shopping in some sectors and how Amazon has spread its offerings from books to a wide range of products from watches to shoes. Conversely, if a distribution method is inconvenient, customers will look elsewhere for the product (or simply not buy). Sometimes inconveniences are tolerated because the need is high or are compensated for by other factors. For example, some people will put up with waiting in line at a store's checkout only because any alternative is too far away or has no convenient car park.

Market maps

Market maps can help in both selecting a channel and in managing disparate channels. They are a graphic representation of the routes a product travels along that can be used to simplify and make more precise the job of channel selection and management, particularly comparison between different channels.

This concept of market maps (originated by Michael T. Wilson in his book *The Management of Marketing*, Gower Publishing, 1989) formalises simple flow charts into a specific form. It aids analysis, planning and implementation, and describes the nature of a system, showing all the channels in existence or use. It can be quantified to show what is happening where.

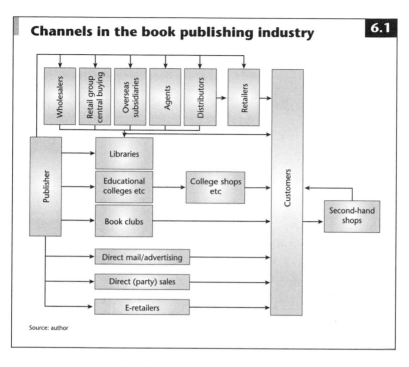

Channels in the book publishing industry 6.1

Source: author

A simple example of the various channels involved in the book publishing industry is illustrated in Figure 6.1. This shows the wide span of possibilities. In reality one company may opt for only a few of these, and most publishers of any size will supply the different channels that eventually lead to the customer mainly through their own distributor or a third-party distributor which also handles invoicing and returns.

A map like this can be used to help choose the right mix and for some products will be even more complex. Preparing a map involves:

▶ listing the categories of consumers or end-users and any subdivisions they may contain;

▶ listing any additional influencers (such as architects who specify building materials);

▶ asking questions about customers and their characteristics so that information is clear alongside how their purchasing relates to the map; for example:

How channels affect marketing approaches

The book market map shows that traditional retailers may judge a textbook in terms of price, how up to date it is, its link with particular courses (a book officially recommended by a university is more likely to be bought and stocked than one just rated as "useful"), its accessibility and so on, and by the reputation, standing and presentation of the publisher and author. The support they need can be provided by a publisher's sales team.

University bookshops may have similar criteria, but academics have a different perspective and need handling differently. Yet they can be approached to try to secure agreement that the book becomes recommended reading. This may increase sales through both university bookshops and larger bookshops with academic departments. The link with such people is, however, radically different from that with typical bookshop buyers of academic titles and needs a different sales approach. But it is a channel that can be identified, an approach can be tailored for it and the information coming from an updated market map can help to identify such situations and to monitor progress.

Marketers must always keep in mind that such distribution strategies need to be reviewed regularly in the light of changes in the marketplace.

- Who are they? (male/female, age, buying power and so on for individuals and comparable information for industrial buyers, such as type of industry)
- What are their needs? (for value, performance, convenience and so on these can be linked specifically to a particular product)
- How are their needs being satisfied? (by both direct and, if relevant, indirect competition)
- Where do they buy? (linking to the different channels featured on the map)

Preparing a map may require assembling a lot of data and making sure that accurate sales figures are produced in the right form; even some research may be useful. With the right set-up – for example computer programs that will convert conventional sales data into "channel form" – much of it can be easily updated. Together, the information and a map to illustrate what is happening will help:

▶ assist planning and setting strategy (which channels to use/not use);

▶ monitor performance (including both sales revenue and costs), allowing fine-tuning of marketing action directed at specific channels;

▶ highlight the relationships involved (which customers use which channels and so on);

▶ allow a view to be taken of matters such as pricing and profitability that reflects what is happening, not in an overall sense, but in the way individual channels work.

The example opposite shows one aspect of the various ways the concept can be used and illustrates how reviewing channels can lead to fundamental changes in marketing approach.

Using stockists or doing it yourself

There are a number of good reasons for using specialist retailers or wholesalers rather than setting up your own retail network. Among the advantages of using established retailers are that they:

▶ provide a ready-made network of contacts that would otherwise take years to establish from scratch at what might be a prohibitive cost. Even a large company might baulk at the cost of setting up its own retail chain and few do;

▶ are objective and are rarely tied to one product or brand, though they may limit themselves to one type of product such as books;

▶ provide an environment that customers need in order to make a choice. If competing brands need to be compared, the customer in an outlet offering a range of similar products can do so conveniently. A retailer that is well known in its own right with an attractive image may enhance the overall attractiveness of the shopping experience in the eyes of a consumer. In many fields allowing potential customers to view a wide choice – as in, say, selecting a television – is an important aspect of encouraging sales. So too is the quality of advice;

▶ can spread the costs of carrying and selling one product over all the items they carry, thereby distributing it at a lower cost than a supplier operating alone;

▶ often offer a range of credit facilities to help customers, and the cost of bad debts is sometimes lower than it would be otherwise because the stockist effectively shares the risk (though slow payment of manufacturers seems endemic in many industries);

▶ are rewarded by a discount off the selling price, and so no capital is tied up by the principal in holding local stocks, though overlong credit can dilute this effect;

▶ can have specialist knowledge of retailing or distribution that the principal may not possess; this varies across different kinds of intermediary.

There can, however, be conflicts of interest between principals and retailers. Potential problems may include the following:

▶ Commitment to your product. A retailer will sell what it can and may be encouraged through higher discounts to promote one product rather than another.

▶ Price cutting that reduces margins and may damage the brand. For instance, retailers may discount products at Christmas or in seasonal sales that producers might feel inappropriate; champagne that normally commands a premium price is an example.

▶ A product being dropped in the belief that more profit can be made from a competing line.

▶ Promotional costs. Sometimes retailers are more interested in the financial support they get to promote a product than what they might earn from selling the product itself.

▶ Tough terms and complex, time-consuming ordering procedures, and a failure to collaborate in ways that might increase sales for both parties.

The question of whether to deal direct with the consumer depends, therefore, first upon the availability of suitable channels and the willingness of buyers within them to add additional products to the range they sell; and second, on balancing the economies of the stockists' lower unit selling and servicing costs with the disadvantages of not being present at the point where customers make their purchasing decisions and thus having less control over the selling process. Realistically, many companies have no option but to go through existing channels, though exactly how this is done and the mix involved can vary. Furthermore, more radical variants may be needed to run alongside (and without alienating) the retailers. Many consumer goods manufacturers also sell their products direct to companies for use as business gifts, as Parker does with its range of pens. If the opportunity to do this exists, it is a good route to increasing business.

Selecting the right distribution channel

There is no one easy and obvious route for most suppliers; indeed, having only one route to market is likely to limit sales. A mix of methods needs to be considered and any decision on which channels to use must be based on fact and analysis. Six main characteristics will influence the decision:

▶ **Customer characteristics.** Retailers are usually required when customers are widely dispersed, there are a large number of them and they buy frequently in small amounts. This is certainly true of many types of everyday products, but less so (or not at all) for some specialist items.

▶ **Product characteristics.** Direct distribution is required for bulky or heavy products. It is crucial to minimise the shipping distance and the number of times products need to be handled; a brief consideration of physical distribution costs shows the importance of this. Where high unit value can cover higher unit selling costs, the manufacturer can keep control over sales by dealing direct, as with off-the-page or catalogue selling or even door-to-door systems. Products such as domestic heating boilers that need be installed or maintained by a specialist are generally sold through a limited network, such as sole agents.

▶ **Distributor characteristics.** Distributors are most useful when their low-cost contacts, service and storage are more important than their lack of commitment to one product or brand. If specific support is needed, other options may be preferable.

▶ **Competitor characteristics.** The channels chosen may often be influenced by the channels competitors use, and there may be dangers in moving away too far and too fast from what a market expects and likes. The competitive interaction between retailers is another variable. Burger King, for example, tries to find sites near to McDonald's outlets. Some manufacturers such as Avon, a global cosmetics company, choose not to compete for scarce positions in retail stores and have established profitable door-to-door direct selling operations instead. Similarly, major chains may seek to open branches near smaller independent retailers, not only to take advantage of their market knowledge – they are in an area where there is a demand – but with the aim of replacing them completely. This may not be in customers' interests and illustrates one aspect of the sheer power of major retailing groups.

▶ **Company characteristics.** A company's size often correlates with its market share – and the bigger its market share, the easier it is to find stockists willing to handle its product(s). Even a small outlet is likely to find a corner for major brands, but it will be more selective about what else it offers. Because it cannot stock everything, it will offer the products that provide the best profit opportunities. Equally, a supplier may be innovative (and/or build on a strength) and seek ways of becoming less dependent on the normal chain of distribution. This may require creativity. For instance, cosmetics may sell well in outlets that simply display them, but stores putting on make-up demonstrations (or letting the manufacturer do so) may create an advantage – for a while.

Additionally, fast delivery is less easily achieved when there are many stages in the channel. This increases the danger of diluting the effectiveness of marketing because customers dislike slow delivery. This is a problem for some e-tailers. The instant nature of buying over the internet prompts consumers to feel that delivery should be swift – a feeling encouraged by those who achieve it. Distance (and, for some people, the still new method) can reduce credibility and trust; one bad experience of delay is enough to rule out any repeat business (especially if resolving any pending matters is difficult, too).

▶ **Environmental characteristics.** Changes in the economic and legal environment can bring about changes in distribution structures. For example, when the market is depressed, manufacturers are prompted to cut out intermediaries or inessential services to compete on price and deal direct. However, legal restrictions exist in some countries to prevent any channel characteristics that may weaken competition.

Overall retail trends must also be considered. Out-of-town shopping, the use of the car (or restrictions on it) and everything from the cost of renting retail premises to the desirability of an area will influence the likelihood of shoppers patronising a particular area and thus a particular shop. This may influence where all sorts of products are bought, and may in turn influence what is bought. There are many other influencing factors, ranging from government monopolies controlling liquor sales in some American states to countries – Africa and Asia, for example – where the only realistic way to break into some sectors is to grease some palms.

A potential customer's first decision may be to visit a particular shopping area. What is there and how they view outlets then influences what customers buy and where they do their buying. Any change to the shopping environment is likely to have repercussions; and doubtless there are many changes still to come.

Variety and change

Usually it is possible to identify several different types of potential distribution channel or stockist. In certain industries some of the alternatives may be further from standard practice than others, but that does not mean they should not be considered or cannot be part of the distribution mix. What is normal now may have originally been difficult to establish. For example, party selling is well known (Tupperware has become a generic word and Avon

Cosmetics is well known in many markets around the world), but some companies use this technique in areas where it is very much not the norm and make it successful, as Usborne Publishing does with children's books.

Some companies are bound to the standard form in their field, but marketers should always remain open minded; channels may change little and traditional routes may remain the most important, creating the greatest volume of business, but other possibilities may still create some growth.

There are doubtless many innovations in prospect for distribution (one need only look at the impact of the internet to see how channels can change dramatically). Everyone has 20/20 hindsight. Suppliers must make sure that some marketing time, effort and thinking go into exploring and testing new methods. This is true of most aspects of marketing, but the route to market is a prime candidate because it is often seen as essentially static, at least in the short term. This must be linked with supply chain management, which has changed radically.

Marketers must explore the alternatives to decide which channel or combination of channels best meets an organisation's objectives and constraints. They must take into account the degree of control or influence the organisation will have over it, but the primary consideration is that it should work well for customers.

Customer service

Brands exist to create superior customer value and thus maximise profit opportunities. Channels have a similar role. They should not just provide a route along which products and services flow, but also actively create availability in a way that provides customers with a satisfactory – indeed, for consumer goods, interesting, perhaps even exciting – way of obtaining what they want.

Channels must be judged on the basis of how well they deliver their "package" of service benefits. So, how a channel provides the following is important:

▶ Convenience – such as how much time is taken up (including, for instance, being nearby, ease of parking and having sensible opening hours). For e-retailers, the attractiveness of the website and how easy it is to find and use are crucial.

▶ Range – choice and mix of products available.

▶ Price – value in price terms includes all aspects of price (for example, discounts and payment terms).

▶ Quality – overall value including price and service.

▶ Service – customer care attitudes and practice and advice if necessary (including indirect service issues such as the provision of washrooms in a shopping mall).

▶ Environment – everything from style to cleanliness, also ease of use (for example, being baby/pushchair friendly) and size of crowds.

▶ Identification – clarity of purpose (for example, are the shops in a mall all high price or the reverse, say "factory outlets" – this clearly identifies what is on offer).

▶ Image – in the overall sense of projecting such things as quality, the kind of person to whom it is directed and so on.

Channels can be segmented just as much as products. A channel may well focus on a part, sometimes a tightly focused part, of a total market. Thus in terms of both price and people channels may be designed to attract in different ways. Customers can, for example, buy a new kitchen packed flat in boxes from a chain store at an out-of-town shopping centre, or have someone visit their home and advise and supply them individually and then install it.

The channel can also be used to enhance image, for example:

▶ Upmarket theme bars featuring more expensive "designer" beers and speciality drinks use the quality or trendy image to tie in with the appeal of individual products.

▶ The restricted availability of a top brand of perfume or fine china, sold only through a small number of exclusive dealerships, enhances the image of desirability.

▶ A humble loaf of bread sold in a small "real" bakery has sufficient value added to its appeal to command a premium price.

The ultimate measure is what works for consumers. A channel will not continue to operate successfully without the approval of the customers who use it (unless they have no alternative, in which case it is vulnerable to new competition).

The power of retailers

When a few companies dominate an area of distribution they wield considerable power. In both the United States and the UK this is dramatically demonstrated in food marketing. Retail sales of any branded food product in the UK go through just four companies whose shops make up 80% of the market. Any manufacturer whose food products are not available in any one of those chains loses a significant chunk of the potential market.

The structure of the market gives the big chains considerable power and to a large degree they call the shots, though individual chains take pains to counter accusations that they abuse their power and that their negotiating stance does not respect suppliers' interests. When a few retailers are so powerful producers' margins are constantly under pressure, and yet they need to support each retailer in a way that maximises their business opportunities in the chain concerned.

When dealing with Tesco or Wal-Mart a manufacturer might be pressed to include:

▶ More time from the sales force (for instance, to help with merchandising).

▶ Discounts (and there may be many different bases for them, such as quantity bought or timing of purchase).

▶ Special packaging and packing.

▶ Delivery (maybe to multiple locations), labelling, credit terms and so on.

▶ Returns and damage arrangements.

▶ Advertising and promotional support.

▶ Merchandising materials.

▶ Training of the retailer's staff.

▶ Financing (including special credit terms, sometimes imposed retrospectively).

These costs are in addition to normal production and distribution costs. Yet, as indicated above, big retail chains can make demands that cut margins, knowing that the supplier is under intense pressure to maintain a relationship with them. Nevertheless, a retailer will not want to alienate a supplier and miss the opportunity of selling a good product profitably. A balance is necessary, even though the supplier may sometimes think it is lopsided.

Large wholesalers and retailers need careful handling: they are not just different in size, they are also different in nature and so require what is called key account management.

Thus the first stage of channel management is to select the right channel or, more likely, to select and balance the right mix of channels. The second is to make the way it is used as effective as possible.

Contractual arrangements

Arrangements with wholesalers and retailers are usually contractual. This is not a legal nicety; it is imperative to make sure the detail is right and, in international operations, that it is right for each market. For instance, a review showed that one European industrial component company trading across the world had 18 different forms of contract in force. This was causing friction between the principal and its distributors and involved costly renegotiation. It is better to set a consistent policy in the first place and have a regular review process in place from the beginning. And who you decide to contract with also matters in terms of price and service commitment levels. For example, a fast-food chain is likely to opt to work with either PepsiCo or Coca-Cola, but not both.

Managing channels

Distribution channels require active management. Not only are chosen wholesalers and retailers likely to work better on behalf of a manufacturer if communications (such as information, training, services, support and motivation) are good, but they will also have their own ideas, and a good working relationship must be created if both are to profit from the partnership. This takes time, and often it is easy to see people as sources of revenue rather than someone to work with. Yet the best may be obtained from a market only when two parties work effectively together.

For example, few retailers will consider taking on a new product (or taking on board an idea) unless they are convinced that demand for it exists. They need to know which market segment the product is aimed at and whether it fits with their customer franchise. The same is true of industrial and other markets.

For a channel of distribution to be successful there must be:

▶ clear policy – all parties must have clear, understood and agreed expectations of each other;

▶ clear terms of trade (discounts and all financial arrangements);

▶ sufficient time and resources available for managing, communicating with and motivating the people upon whom sales ultimately depend.

Communications, motivation and support are crucial, and must not be approached ad hoc. All need a systematic approach, well tailored to the people on the receiving end especially if, for example, widespread global networks add to the complexity.

In selecting and managing channels of distribution, the following must happen:

▶ Analysis of the market as a whole, how it operates and how it can, and might, be accessed.

▶ Analysis of individual distribution channels to see how they fit with marketing activity and marketing strategy.

▶ Analysis of how well the channels meet customer needs.

▶ Selection of the right mix.

▶ Prioritisation of the channels in terms of the flow of business through each and the respective weight of activity that will be put behind it.

▶ Agreement of satisfactory (contractual) arrangements with the parties involved (wholesalers, retailers and so on).

▶ Creation and maintenance of a relationship with them through an appropriate communications programme.

▶ The planning and implementation of individual key account strategies with customers who warrant attention at this level.

▶ Performance reviews and fine-tuning activity as necessary.

▶ The investigation of new channels and new ways of making existing channels work more effectively in future.

Ultimately sales are made at the interface between the manufacturer and the stockist, whatever form that takes. So the supplier must work effectively with the way things are (despite wishing they were different), and also seek to find new approaches and methods that will lead to more effective distribution.

Approaches that make distribution work

Channel management involves taking a marketing approach to distribution. Decisions about what to do are important, but so too is what is done to make distribution work and that too defines managing channels.

Making the selection

There are various factors to balance, including customers and different customer types; product characteristics; stockist characteristics (literally what skills and resources they "bring to the party"); competition; and the question of what is best done by the principal or the stockist.

Research and analysis may be necessary and some options that may not seem so far apart (for example, exclusive or non-exclusive agents or dealers) may have important differences that demand investigation to enable the right choice to be made.

Many options also have legal consequences, so care before signing any agreement is essential. The main processes in making a selection are:

▶ reviewing a wide range of options;

▶ gathering the necessary information;

▶ taking time to study the options and the information that exists about them.

For companies operating internationally, this process may need to be repeated for each geographic market.

Choosing the channel mix

As stated earlier, channel choice is not just a matter of picking the route to market; that is right for only a few organisations. Rather, it involves picking a mix of channels that make sense and then deciding the relative importance of each.

This does not mean simply ranking them; it means making decisions about the investment in each and forecasting what each will do. A market map helps to clarify what may be a complex picture. The chosen channel mix must reflect a clear strategy for each channel. As different channels may be used for widely different purposes, they must all be managed to achieve their own particular objectives.

For example, tyre manufacturers can sell through two completely different channels. One may aim to sell to car manufacturers, which need tyres as original equipment. The other may aim to sell replacement tyres to car owners. The two routes need different approaches: one to access the comparatively small number of motor manufacturers; the other to access the numerous and different kinds of outlets selling replacement tyres.

In choosing the mix, decisions need to be made on which channels to use for what (and which not to use), how to maximise the effectiveness of each channel and the priorities of the different routes involved. As stated earlier, the choice is almost always a compromise, but customer satisfaction is the overriding issue; everything else must take account of it.

Managing the channels

When the routes have been chosen, people along them need to be influenced. Managing the channels in this sense means:

▶ incorporating specific channel-focused activity into the marketing plan;

▶ setting clear priorities for making each channel work;

▶ allocating people appropriately (for example, who will be accountable for the customers in different channels and how will these customers be serviced – as illustrated by the car tyre example);

▶ creating and maintaining appropriate service back-up for each channel (and for each kind of customer, including the ultimate user).

It also includes supply chain management: matching a range of activities to the nature of particular channels and customers. For example, transport and distribution need the right size trucks for deliveries to particular kinds of customer; change this and the fleet may be rendered obsolete.

Effective communication along supply chains is also crucial to success. It must sell to customers and create, maintain and develop relationships with them; this links to account management.

This communication may use every available method, from e-mail to video-conferencing, and it must be planned and sustained (and therefore budgeted for in both time and money). It is all too easy for marketers to think that just because a product sells well, a contract exists, and if advertising is good, people along a supply chain will effectively promote and sell the product unbidden. Rather, success in managing channels effectively demands a systematic and creatively executed communications programme with clear objectives.

Channels and markets

Channels are dynamic and can change rapidly, therefore people in different markets see things differently and expect their viewpoints to be understood and respected by their suppliers. All activity must be tailored to individual channels. This is easier when the channels are very different (as in the car tyre example), but it needs careful thought when the differences are less obvious.

For example, an international brand of chocolate may appear essentially the same in Bangkok, Boston and Brussels. But in all likelihood it is not. It must have a higher melting point when sold in hot countries. It might be possible to sell the standard version in hot climates (it could be transported in refrigerated containers), but it must also survive local distribution – it might be that no one will handle it unless it does, because the local distributors will get any complaints. Everything – which includes a plethora of features from assembly instructions to packaging (both needing translation internationally) – must relate to the market and thus to the channel.

Thus the decision-making process and management relating to channels are more about fitting products to channels than fitting channels to (existing) products. It is crucial to achieve an effective fit. Other marketing activity, such as advertising, must also fit. This may need to:

▶ incorporate channel information to make it clear how something can be purchased;

▶ be directed not only at the ultimate consumer but also at intermediaries along the supply chain.

Advertising must always be appropriate and well directed to its target audience. Different strategies are involved: some international brands use the same advertising worldwide (for example, HSBC with its "The world's local bank" campaign); others focus on different markets in different ways. No matter how it is done, successful advertising helps people walk into a sales outlet already feeling strongly that one brand is right for them, and perhaps with a preconditioned frame of mind to accept no substitutes. Whatever the circumstances, marketing activity must fit with the way methods of distribution are organised.

Fine-tuning channel performance

A channel is not for life. Given that what is being implemented is a mix, it is a prime part of channel management to monitor the comparative performance of all channels in order to:

▶ improve the way each channel performs;

▶ better balance the mix, putting more emphasis on one channel and reducing it on another;

▶ (perhaps) change radically the way distribution is handled.

The quick and easy way to review this is by using a market map (see page 74).

For whatever reason, the overall aspects of channel selection and management seem to remain untouched longer than many other aspects of marketing. This is likely to leave an organisation open to danger and at risk of missing opportunities. Review should be a regular and structured process, and new developments should be observed and innovative options sought.

Sometimes organisations make substantial changes such as embarking on widening their distribution through e-commerce. In practice, many changes are minor – evolution is more common than revolution – but that does not mean that they are not worthwhile. They may well be – and a series of them may be even more useful.

International dimensions

If a business operates internationally, the principles outlined here are equally applicable. Additionally, it will be important to:

▶ fit methodology to markets – this may involve a variety of routes across different countries or territories, all of which suit the local culture;

▶ not allow distance and difficulties such as language to affect adversely the need to support and motivate distributors (whatever form they may take);

▶ not infringe the local legal system – this may affect the contract made with an independent distributor, for instance;

▶ keep everything manageable – the wider the network and the more organisations and people it involves, the more difficult it is to maintain suitable communications.

Despite the difficulties involved, increasing the number of places where a product is sold is a classic option for building a business, and this can be achieved successfully only through a clear distribution strategy. Making channel management successful is much the same as making any aspect of marketing successful. If the principles of good channel management are well applied, it can contribute positively to the marketing process and, in so doing, help to provide a positive edge in the market.

Key points

This chapter describes an element of marketing that is wide in its implications and operations. It:

▶ overlaps other organisational functions, such as physical distribution, and demands consideration for both the short and long term;

▶ is regarded by some organisations, and some marketing people, as fixed, or at least not as likely to yield to analysis and action to change and update current practice in a way that influences results positively as do other areas of marketing – yet it must be regarded as dynamic, since marketing is essentially a creative process;

▶ has been influenced substantially by technical change and development in recent years, especially by the internet.

In distribution channels, as much as in other areas, change needs to be marketing led to find and exploit the best method of operating and linking to markets.

3

Strategy and marketing planning

Marketing strategy

*If you don't know where you're going, it's
really hard to get there.*

Viri Mullins, president, Armstrong's Lock & Supply

A prerequisite of marketing success is being clear about what marketing activity aims to achieve and how it will achieve it. Only then can marketing activity be organised and implemented. Strategy sets out the way in which action will proceed to achieve results. And strategy can be set only in the light of information: in the context of the way marketing works in terms of information about an organisation, its product and its markets. This may well come in part from research – and certainly from analysis.

This implies compiling a marketing plan, which is a crucial part of making marketing successful. As Malcolm McDonald, former professor of marketing and deputy director at Cranfield School of Management, says in his book *On Marketing Planning*: "The purpose of marketing planning is the identification and creation of competitive advantage."

A basis for success

The initial plan (and the planning process, which is dealt with in Chapter 8) will indicate a number of options, possibly many over all the stages it considers. Next decisions must be made that provide a strategic focus on when and how the marketing effort should be applied.

Three levels of decision-making are involved:

▶ Defining the market (the group of customers/potential customers with whom an organisation hopes, or rather intends, to do business; this may be complicated by any international dimension).

▶ Setting clear objectives (the desired results in the chosen marketplace).

▶ Selecting strategic direction (the course of action that is intended to achieve those results).

These three levels may seem obvious, but that is because they are fundamental to success. In any organisation, especially one without dramatic product advantages, the clarity and focus given to marketing often determine the level of success it achieves. Thus companies such as Starbucks, which expanded fast and successfully, almost always have a clarity of purpose that gives strength to everything they do both in marketing and those elements that support it (for example, staff motivation in the case of Starbucks).

The market

The definition of the current and intended market is often difficult. If it is too narrow, a company's marketing strategy may also be too narrow and fail to achieve the product's potential. If it is too wide, the marketing strategy and resources may be too diffuse, again failing to achieve the product's potential. The problem stems from the fact that the concept of "market" has many interpretations. A market may be:

▶ a group of people sharing a common interest (car drivers, computer buffs, doctors, training managers);

▶ a particular part of the world (Manchester, New York City, Granada TV area, the Middle East, the southern sales region, the European Union, South-East Asia);

▶ a broad business sector (information technology);

▶ a narrow business sector (dictionaries within the total book market);

▶ a particular product area that cuts across many market segments (computers).

Deciding what market an organisation is (or should be) in is strategically crucial and is to a large extent determined by an intelligent and objective marketing view of the business. This will dictate – or at least guide – the marketing strategy, product development and pricing policies.

Having identified the market segments in which it is competing, an organisation has to assess how its products, their presentation and their packaging match the characteristics of the chosen segments. In doing so, a company has to recognise it has the choice of targeting four broad market types:

▶ Undifferentiated markets, in which a blanket, take it or leave it marketing package that covers just about everyone likely to buy a product will suffice. The risk of this strategy is that it ignores the fact that consumers make choices and enjoy doing so, and so can be dangerous because it leaves products open to attack by competitors attempting to seize sub-segments by appealing more closely to specific segment needs.

▶ Concentrated markets, in which services or products are closely matched with the needs of a narrow market segment. Being a big fish in a small pool has many advantages, especially for smaller organisations lacking the resources to compete in much broader or multiple markets. This specialist approach also has disadvantages. If there is a business downturn in one narrow segment, the company may lack a sufficiently broad base of alternative buyers to whom resources can be quickly redirected to create new sales.

▶ Differentiated markets, which are a compromise between the two extremes above. This marketing approach looks at the entire range of segments within a particular market and seeks to satisfy those of sufficient size and potential reward with precisely targeted but similar products. For example, Volvo Penta manufactures diesel engines for leisure boats. Within that closely defined market it has a model for every significant segment from sailing yachts to 50-metre luxury cruisers.

▶ Served (or existing) markets imply little purposeful planning. Organisations are led into sectors by market opportunities, perhaps in an unco-ordinated manner, rather than devising a co-ordinated strategy to take them into the most advantageous sectors. In other words, they are opportunity led rather than strategy driven.

Even with apparently simple products, different markets can be involved. For example, a company selling beds to consumers, hotels, hospitals and prisons is spanning a wide area where different considerations apply.

With a clear view of the target market, marketers can turn to setting objectives.

Marketing objectives and strategies

Clear objectives exist to focus and to place any tactical activities in order of priority. Clear means quantified wherever possible (rather than all-embracing statements such as: "We will aim to make as much money as possible"). A much-quoted mnemonic shows whether this has been achieved. Objectives should be SMART, that is, specific, measurable, achievable, realistic and timed (see Chapter 8).

Beyond that, the overall objectives available to succeed and grow in the market must be considered in the light of the strategies that will be deployed. Surprisingly, there are just six overall objectives:

▶ Increase the share of the existing market (necessarily winning business from competitors) by concentrating on selected segments, developing product applications and using different brand names.

▶ Expand existing markets by increasing the frequency of customer purchase, increasing usage and opening new branches.

▶ Develop new markets for existing products or services through approaching new market segments and export marketing.

▶ Devise new products or services for existing markets by revising old products and introducing radically new ones.

▶ Create new products or services in new markets through

diversification, takeover and technological extension, improving the value offered to customers, marketing audit and productivity improvement and such tactics as reducing the range.

▶ Increase the profitability of existing markets by improving value to customers or any means possible, such as increasing productivity, adjusting the product range or fine-tuning promotional activity to improve its effectiveness.

These options are not mutually exclusive. Often a combination will produce even greater marketing success. However, the danger for an organisation is to adopt too many courses of action, spreading marketing resources too thinly and failing to put sufficient effort behind the prime options.

Whichever options are chosen, it is crucial that the marketing strategy:

▶ satisfies the needs of the various precise target groups at which it is aimed – consumers, wholesalers, customers and so on;

▶ achieves the corporate marketing, financial and growth objectives;

▶ gives direction to various elements of marketing activity products, prices, distribution and promotion;

▶ blends well with any other marketing or general business strategies, in others words it does not hinder their achievement;

▶ capitalises on the corporate strengths and minimises the effect of any weaknesses;

▶ creates a competitive advantage that is difficult to match or surpass;

▶ is within the competence and resources of the company.

Decisions must also be made about positioning: the place selected within the range of options represented by the market. For example, Volvo cars are widely viewed as safe, BMW offers "the ultimate driving machine" and Porsche says it makes the best small sports cars in the world. All are positioned differently from each other in the market; something that is separate from their size, profitability or other measures that might be applied to them.

The nature of a product is usually considered to be the most important element of the total marketing mix. Based on the marketing objectives and strategies of a company, management must make a variety of decisions on product mix, product lines, brands and services. These decisions are central to the company's prosperity and it is therefore important to assess, relative to the competition, how well products perform in terms of the needs they aim to satisfy.

In evaluating product performance marketers must recognise that products are bought for what they do rather than for what they are; that the benefits conferred by a product stem not only from actual physical features, but also from a collection of other characteristics (both objective and subjective) such as availability, reputation, after-sales service and fit with lifestyle. Seemingly small changes can influence sales too. For example, Tetley made major gains when it introduced the first round tea bag and Dutch Boy similarly increased paint sales with an improved easy-pour container. While the container gave a practical reason for success, the round tea bag shows how marketing is as much an art as a science: was it successful because it makes better tea or because of image and the scope it offered for successful promotion? Possibly both. What matters is that customers felt there was an advantage.

In many markets, especially but not only consumer ones, the brand, that is the product name, is crucial in terms of what is called brand image. This is the product and all that goes with it. So the brand image of, say, an airline includes everything from the service, the fares, the livery and check-in arrangements, as well as behind-the-scenes elements such as maintenance and safety procedures, to the name and the way everything is presented in promotion and advertising. Companies must decide what brand image they want to create and then make sure that all management decisions are taken in ways that build and support that image. Sometimes the desired brand image is wide, all things to all people; sometimes it is narrow, designed to appeal to a particular niche market. In many fields different organisations have very different images, for instance Apple and IBM. Sometimes the brand name becomes a generic description, as with Hoover, Kleenex, Thermos and Biro.

This makes the brand easily recognisable and gives it an advantage in the customer's decision-making process about which product to buy.

Product life-cycle

In selecting strategies, it is important to bear in mind two things:

▶ The cost of launching a new product is considerable and the certainty of success low. Even top companies can fail: PepsiCo spent $100m launching Pepsi One only to quickly withdraw it; Xerox is no longer a name in computers.

▶ The failure rate is high; in fast-moving consumer goods (FMCG) markets, only one in ten new products survive any length of time.

Often the first launch is in a test market. Instead of launching nationally, the product is tried out in a small region, a state, a county or a television region (if TV advertising is planned). This may reduce the risk, but even then there are other things to consider:

▶ When – if the product is replacing an existing one, should stocks of the old product be run down? If demand is seasonal and the season is well advanced, should the launch be postponed until next season?

▶ Where – an area must be chosen where rapid acceptance and pay-back can be achieved rather than launching it in the main stronghold of a competitor.

▶ To whom – certain sections of the population are often more open to new ideas than others and so are willing to try it. These should be targeted first, especially with such things as IT products.

▶ How – a clear promotion strategy needs to be planned to get public relations, advertising and selling to reinforce each other and produce optimum results.

The progressive launch of a movie around the world will change as experience in one location influences what is done elsewhere. A clear path of action is needed despite the complexities involved in creating a clear strategy. Various approaches can assist the analysis and decision-making.

Analysis as the basis of strategic planning

Several approaches can help to cut through the complexity. Their role is to organise and arrange information so that good decisions can be made, making the best possible results more likely. No single plan or strategy is "right". All that can be done is to make sure that the decision is made on a well-considered basis and that as many pertinent facts as possible are known when this is done. The best known and perhaps most useful formal approach is SWOT analysis.

SWOT analysis

SWOT stands for strengths and weaknesses, opportunities and threats. The technique formalises a common-sense view of what needs to be investigated early in the planning process before strategies are set. It is a classic means to an end. SWOT analysis prompts the questions that should sensibly be asked at this stage. These may need investigation before they can be satisfactorily answered, and the answers may need some analysis before what they are really saying becomes clear.

Diligently addressed, the process ensures that planning can proceed on the basis of a sound knowledge of the strengths and weaknesses within an organisation and the opportunities and threats that exist externally. Some answers will be obvious and well known. Others will not, and investigation may produce surprises. Even one significant area of sound information being flagged may affect action materially. If such an analysis has never been undertaken in the past, it will take some time. But on an annual basis (planning usually being an annual cycle), it is not a daunting part of the total process to update the analysis; and it is certainly useful.

SWOT analysis is best explained through the sorts of questions it involves, which can be applied to products or services in any sort of organisation (see opposite).

An organisation's strengths and weaknesses

Customer base

What is the current customer base, by size, by location, by category?

How does the disposition of the company's customers (customer mix) compare with the wider market mix?

Are existing customers in market(s) that are growing?

How far (as a specific measurement) does the organisation depend on its largest customers?

Range of products or services

How closely does the product range reflect the market's needs?

How does the product range compare with competitors'?

Are most existing areas of business in growth or decline?

Is the span of the product range too narrow to satisfy existing markets?

Or is the product range too broad to allow satisfactory management of performance across the range?

Price structure

What is the basis of pricing policy?

Do direct and indirect competitors structure their prices in the same way?

Are current prices competitive?

Do customers perceive existing prices as offering "value for money"?

Promotional and selling activities

Which customer groups are communications directed at?

What do these people know and feel about the organisation?

Are communications directed at sufficient numbers of the "right" people (both groups and individuals)?

What means of communication are being used?

What attitudes exist internally that influence approaches to promotion and selling?

Is each person in contact with customers capable of selling the full range and doing so equally well for every element of it?

Do customer contact staff possess the necessary knowledge and skill to sell successfully?

Planning marketing activity

Do agreed plans for marketing and selling exist?

Do the plans state specific activities as well as objectives and budgets? Are they measurable and able to be monitored?

Are there individual or departmental plans as well as corporate plans?

Organising for marketing

How is the organisation's marketing activity organised and co-ordinated?

Are authority and responsibility for each person or activity clearly defined?

Are all employees committed to contributing to a marketing culture that will assist in achieving commercial success?

Control and measurement of marketing

Is "success" defined and communicated to staff?

Are all the necessary significant result areas to measure that success identified?

Do these standards examine marketing as well as corporate goals and standards?

Is performance measured against desired standards and is appropriate (and prompt) corrective action taken?

Market opportunities and threats

How is the market structured quantitatively?

How many people or organisations of what type are there in the market with a need for this kind of product?

What are their current buying practices?

How much do they spend on such items?

How often do they buy (for example, annually or monthly)?

Who do they buy from currently?

What do they not buy?

How do existing and potential buyers access the market and buy similar products?

How is the market structured qualitatively?

Why do existing and potential customers buy/not buy?

What do they think of what they buy (for example, good value or overpriced)?

What do they think of those who supply their current needs (for example, too big, too small, helpful, unhelpful)?

How is the market served competitively?

Who are direct competitors (that is, other similar companies)?

Who are indirect competitors (that is, "overlapping" companies, some of which it may be easy to overlook as not competing)?

What are their strengths and weaknesses (for example, size, staff, image, pricing, marketing skills, geographic coverage)?

What are the quantitative and qualitative trends?

Market or segment size.

Market or segment requirements.

Market or segment structure.

Market or segment location

Competition.

A SWOT analysis is an invaluable tool in helping marketers to chart a course into the future, and it should be seen as part of the concept of a "rolling" plan, which builds on the past as it moves on to the next year and beyond – five, ten or more years.

Using the information

The questions listed on pages 103–5 are a starting point. They indicate the sort of thinking and information needed for an effective marketing strategy to be drawn up, though every company must of course tailor its approach – and the questions it asks – according to the size and nature of the company and the markets in which it operates. For example, customers can be defined in different ways. If an organisation sells direct or only to one industry sector, the power of the retail chains may be of no concern.

Further planning aids are available, such as the Boston Consulting Group's product portfolio analysis, the Ansoff matrix and Michael Porter's five forces model. All are designed to help analyse markets and thus plan how to approach them. Some may be more academic than practical, but whatever method is used must assist the planning process. All the marketing gurus, of whom Philip Kotler is one of the best known, have written extensively about planning and strategy. His book *Kotler on Marketing* is briefer than some, and gives an overview of his thinking.

The scope of planning

Marketers must also consider the level of planning, the lowest being planning related to individual customers. One of the applications of the 80–20 rule (the Pareto Principle) is that 80% of revenue and profit is likely to come from about 20% of a company's customers; this is true for many organisations, though not for retail chains, for instance. This demonstrates that large customers are different from smaller ones and that, while small customers are important, major customers warrant substantial attention because losing one would have a much more damaging effect on the business than losing, say, 100 small customers.

Two things are important here. The first is to flag up opportunities in major customers and help plan sales strategies to exploit them. The second is to analyse customer profitability.

Marketing strategy should be directed at creating positive relationships - partnerships even - with major customers, to make sure that business is maximised. When customers are large organisations it is important to think about opportunities that may be missed. For instance, a training consultant might find that different departments buy different courses: sales by the sales department, business writing by the human resources department and so on. If the significant turnover from a big customer is split in this way, gaps may show up. There may be good reason for them, or they may represent an opportunity and need a change of sales tactics that can be linked into, and specified in, the plan.

Planning to protect and increase customer profitability

Any organisation that analyses the costs of obtaining business may be shocked at just how many factors conspire to reduce margin. They include sales and distribution costs and discounts (and the discount structure can be complicated), as well as special packing, delivery (maybe to multiple locations), labelling, credit terms, advertising and promotional support, merchandising assistance, training of customers' staff - the list goes on. With large, demanding customers margins can be cut to the bone and there is a danger that after overheads a business can become unprofitable.

Thus management must identify possible "profit diluters". For example, it may be that policy is at fault and profit is being lost because published terms need attention, or that policy is right but sales people are failing to achieve sales targets as a result of poor negotiating skills.

A variety of techniques must be considered, but what is done must be a practical compromise that allows planning to take place and reflects the needs of a business. The example below shows how radical planning (and the thinking it entails) can change an organisation's nature.

The change wrought by this kind of thinking is clear; all that is

How planning can create positive change

"What business are we in?" may seem a basic question, but asking it regularly is a good idea as it acts as a reminder and also helps an organisation to recognise how the world has changed and therefore how it needs to change.

A scaffolding company, a traditional business, when asked what business it was in, would originally have replied (seeing it as self-evident): scaffolding for the building industry. True enough, though by its nature this is a current or historic description and somewhat limiting.

Looking ahead, and searching for markets beyond building, the company found that other areas of construction (as varied as chemical plants and offshore oil rigs) needed scaffolding. The description shifted to scaffolding for the construction industry, and the organisation changed to take advantage of these additional opportunities.

So far so good: but what was it the company really sold? Discussion defined this as being temporary access and support. Now a little way from the original description of the business, this led to further searches for market opportunities and inroads being made within the leisure industry, where large amounts of scaffolding are used in temporary spectator stands at events such as music festivals, sports competitions and parades.

Taking this thinking still further, the company found that technically its systems (joints, fixing and so on) were little different from those of its competitors, but concluded that it did have an edge in the skill with which it was able to erect and dismantle scaffolding in terms of speed and safety. While the company had never seen export markets as a possibility (steel tube is prohibitively expensive to transport overseas), expertise can be exported. After further work – shifts of this kind are not achieved without time, effort and investment – the firm developed a profitable business in training others (for instance in the Middle East) to erect and dismantle scaffolding to the same high standards.

needed is to set aside time for constructive thought. Setting strategies and planning may seem like a chore, but they can pay dividends.

Key points

A huge range of planning approaches and techniques can be deployed to set market strategy. It is crucial that:

▶ there are clear objectives, as without them there is no basis for deciding any strategy;

▶ the chosen strategy is well considered and based on as many objective facts about the business as possible;

▶ analysis is a core part of the thinking (whichever and however many techniques may be used to focus it);

▶ final decisions about strategy are based first and foremost on a market view (not just on what is convenient to the organisation);

▶ all this thinking dovetails neatly into a formal and systematic planning process (see Chapter 8);

▶ the essentially creative basis of marketing is not forgotten. There is no "right" way forward, and sometimes success is achieved by those whose planning and setting of strategies unashamedly includes some true inspiration. For example, whoever first sold the gilet (a winter coat with no sleeves) or used a whole sentence as a brand name ("I can't believe it isn't butter") was initially taking a risk.

Marketing planning

The problem is never how to get new
innovative thoughts into the mind, but how to
get the old ones out.

Dee Hock, CEO emeritus, Visa

Cynics say that planning is only anticipating the inevitable and
then taking the credit for it. In reality it is much more than that, and
a (good) marketing plan is essential in creating business success.
Marketing success in a complex world cannot be left to chance,
whatever the size of the business. A small business's marketing
plan might fill one sheet of paper; a large business may need plans
that set out matters in relation to a range of different products and
their intended performance in many different, perhaps global,
markets.

Good reasons for having a plan

The marketing planning process demands a creative approach, yet
it must be based on information and analysis that identifies the
actions to be taken to produce the results budgeted for or desired.
Marketing has many options for action, not least the marketing
plan, which specifies the actions that will be taken (bearing in
mind that as resources are always limited, no organisation can do
everything).

The plan must recognise and balance:

▶ the needs of the organisation;

▶ the needs of its staff (and other groups such as shareholders);

▶ the demands of the external environment and the market (customers);

▶ the activities of competitors;

▶ the resources and capabilities of the organisation.

To be of practical benefit, the plan must:

▶ identify opportunities for future profit improvement;

▶ have the ability to anticipate dynamic external changes;

▶ provide better protection for the future of the business;

▶ prompt the collection of relevant data;

▶ allocate the organisation's resources towards specific ends;

▶ underpin the process of control;

▶ assist with clear communications around the company;

▶ focus individual efforts and assist personal motivation;

▶ provide a proper commercial reference for all activities;

▶ justify development (and development funds).

Additionally, when preparing the plan, it will help if:

▶ the approach adopted is both "bottom up" and "top down" (that is, it involves people throughout the organisation);

▶ the planning system and purpose are clear to all;

▶ standard (tailored) planning formats are used;

▶ a planning cycle, specifying all timings, is agreed (and starts well in advance);

▶ there is a facility to fine tune the plan (particularly to take advantage of opportunities).

Someone must take responsibility for the planning process (and devote time to it), and other people must be involved as necessary. Discipline is required as other pressures easily intrude. Every aspect of the process matters, but the promotional aspects – the things that will bring in the business – are crucial. Marketing, in the guise of the marketing director or manager, must be responsible;

if no such specialist is available (in a small company), the burden falls on the managing director.

The specifics of the marketing plan

The starting point should be to have a clear overall view of the business. Examining the specific content of the marketing plan helps to illustrate why it is important and what it can do.

Revenue can come only from outside an organisation, so how markets are addressed is paramount. The plan overview must specify the elements it should contain and what it should address. Marketing plans should usually include:

▶ a statement of basic assumptions regarding likely future developments (for example, in short/long-term economic, technological and social changes);

▶ a review of past sales (revenue and profit) in as much detail (individual product, market, geography and even major customers) as seems useful;

▶ a statement of the external opportunities and threats;

▶ an analysis of the organisation's strengths and weaknesses in terms of, for example, facilities, human resources and skills, finances, customer franchise; any sound parallel competitive information is also useful;

▶ a statement of long-term objectives and the strategies for achieving them;

▶ a detailed statement of the objectives and strategies for the year ahead, taking this to whatever level is appropriate (that is, individual product, market and elements of marketing activity);

▶ a preview of how the plan for the following year will need to pick up from this year's (and for years beyond that, depending on the organisation's scale of operation);

▶ a statement of priorities showing what is important to the plan and how the organisation will capitalise on its opportunities and identify and correct any weaknesses.

What is needed is a specific action plan that states:

▶ What will be done.

▶ Who will do what.

▶ When and why (in terms of timing implications) actions will be taken.

This applies to every aspect of marketing (including public relations, advertising and promotion, sales and so on). Above all, activity needs to link tightly to the budgets and financial statements. The plan must include the specific actions that will prompt success.

A good starting point, before beginning to assemble the plan, can be to refer to the business's mission statement or to draw one up if no such statement exists.

Mission statements

These are succinct, but all-embracing, statements about a business and its role, purpose and goals. Many mission statements are jargon-filled and vacuous, but a thoughtful and finely judged one helps to provide focus for every function in a business.

It is not so much having a mission statement that is important, although a meaningful one does have considerable merit in helping to enthuse employees, customers and shareholders and give a sense that the organisation knows what it is doing and what it is trying to achieve. Rather, it is the ability to construct one that is crucial. Mission statements both influence and are influenced by the marketing side of the business. Preparing a mission statement is a logical first step in the overall business planning process. It can be devalued by being turned into a public relations statement, which may result in something that sounds nice but will be less useful for planning purposes. Specifically, a mission statement should:

▶ define the kind of business the organisation is in;

▶ identify aspects of business that current plans exclude;

▶ focus on customers, specific customer categories and customer benefits;

▶ link benefits to stakeholders (shareholders, owners and, not least, employees);

▶ say something about the organisation's culture and values (these may be an important part of the firm's profile, as with the Co-operative Bank's environmental attitudes).

Thus McDonald's mission statement has been quoted as:

> Our mission is to be the world's best "quick service restaurant". This means opening and running great restaurants and providing exceptional service, cleanliness and value, so that we can make every customer in every restaurant smile.

These two short sentences spell out much about the nature and scope of the intended business. It was defining the business of Virgin Atlantic as "entertainment" that led to many of its innovations (such as on-board massages).

It is crucial to recognise that a mission statement does not reflect a solely internal view; it must describe the organisation primarily in terms of its outside involvements with markets and customers.

The heart of the plan

Five deceptively simple questions define the planning process, illustrate its logic and dictate what must be done to accomplish it:

▶ Where are we now? This is answered through research and analysis, sometimes called "situation analysis".

▶ Where are we likely to be (at a particular future time)? This is answered by forecasting, whether through an intelligent guesstimate or sophisticated statistical techniques such as regression analysis.

▶ Where do we want to be? The objectives – what is to be achieved and by when.

▶ How will we get there? The action plan for achieving the objectives.

▶ How will it be clear that what happens is on track and, ultimately, that the objectives have been achieved? This reflects the need for management control and control systems as well as real life – no plan can be a wholly accurate description of what will happen. It is designed to be as accurate as possible and essentially more like a route map than a straitjacket. It must allow for fine-tuning and even more substantial changes if they are later felt necessary or in response to unanticipated events.

Compiling the marketing plan

The planning process requires a clear, well-defined and systematic approach. The principles of the process described here are common; the detail of what a marketer needs to do must be tailored to each organisation.

Initial analysis

Writing a plan demands knowledge of the markets in which the business operates and clear marketing objectives. The planners should have the power to authorise or recommend action to agreed cost levels. All companies should have financial goals expressed in revenue and expenditure budgets (in the overall business plan); the task is to translate the financial objectives into market objectives. These must answer the question: what results must be achieved in the marketplace to produce the financial objective required?

The SWOT analysis discussed in Chapter 7 is helpful here. Although the detail may be considerable (and will need documenting), this just means taking a hard, objective look both inside and outside the organisation before setting down more of the plan.

Setting objectives and strategies

Without objectives, it is impossible to place any tactical activities in order of priority. Yet the main marketing objectives (as outlined in Chapter 7) are limited primarily to:

▶ increasing the share of the existing market;

▶ expanding existing markets;

▶ developing new markets for existing products or services;

▶ devising new products or services for existing markets;

▶ creating new products or services in new markets.

From the analysis of market opportunities and threats and the internal assessment of strengths and weaknesses, the marketing objectives that will best achieve the desired financial goals can be selected.

Next, objectives must be linked to strategy, the purpose of which is to focus effort, co-ordinate action and exploit the identified strengths of the organisation and avoid wasting resources on peripheral and non-productive activities. Different objectives may require different strategies, and the result must be well-matched objectives and strategies.

Marketing planning must result in the choice of the most appropriate focus for an organisation's marketing effort. Clarity of focus makes it easier to come up with the tactical marketing plans which cover the range of products or services to be offered, the prices to be charged and the promotional and selling actions to be taken.

Accommodating products and price

As planning continues and time passes, there are broad issues to be considered, such as product life-cycle and positioning. Specifically, companies must recognise that products need to be changed or updated and must keep pace with the market. Price levels must also be monitored for profitability and competitiveness.

Important considerations include the following:

▶ Products or services may remain the same in principle as they were years ago, but they will have to change to meet changing customer needs (as Swiss watchmaker Swatch does by regularly introducing new designs).

▶ New products or services may have to be developed both to meet new customer needs and to keep out competitors.

▶ There may well be opportunities to offer a range of differently priced variants for different customers and different situations (as Japanese watchmaker Seiko does with its sub-brand Avia).

▶ As a harsh economic climate forces corporate customers to seek productivity improvements in all functions of their business, so they become more demanding, but these pressures may also produce new opportunities. For example, a retailer may seek a lower price, but respond well to a supplier that can act to help increase sales, perhaps through merchandising support.

On pricing policy ask:

▶ How aware are customers of price – the actual levels or such measures as hourly rates (for example, for car servicing)?

▶ How do customers perceive price? Do they view, for example, a higher price as indicating higher quality or do they view price as a commodity factor with no differentiation between brands?

▶ Are there "price barriers" in customers' minds for what they are being offered? For example, is $10 or $100 the limit of what they will pay for a particular product?

▶ How far can price be differentiated because of the perceived and accepted reputation that exists?

Price is crucial in the marketing mix and often receives too little attention because the decision made is simply to keep in line with the competition or to work essentially on a cost-plus basis. Price should reflect a company's overall strategy but permit some tactical flexibility to move up or down depending on the threat or opportunity.

The promotion plan

Successful promotional activity needs to be based on a continuous process of review and action that involves not only tried and tested promotional methods but also a willingness to experiment so as to avoid relying on a standard range of preferred options that can become stale. Some of what is involved in a systematic approach to promotional activity is discussed in the next section.

A systematic approach to promotional activity

Twelve planning tasks are listed below and then examined in more detail. Marketers must:

▶ Analyse the market and clearly identify the exact need.

▶ Make sure the need is real and not imaginary and that support is necessary.

▶ Establish that the intended tactics are likely to be the most cost-effective.

▶ Define clear and precise objectives.

▶ Analyse the tactics available, taking into consideration issues regarding:

- the market;
- the target audience;
- the products or services offered;
- the firm's organisation and resources.

▶ Select the mix of tactics to use.

▶ Check budgets to make sure funds are available.

▶ Prepare a written plan of operations.

▶ Discuss and agree the plan with all concerned and obtain permission to proceed.

▶ Communicate the details of the campaign to those involved in implementing it and make sure that they fully understand what they must do and when.

▶ Implement the campaign, ensuring continuous feedback on the information required to monitor performance.

▶ Analyse the results, showing exactly what has happened, what factors affected the results (if any) and how much the activities cost.

Analyse organisational needs

The prime difficulty in the analytical stage is not so much identifying the need, but making sure that it is real and not imaginary. A need can be identified through:

▶ formal, and informal, research;

▶ internal company investigation;

▶ staff;

▶ specific market demands;

▶ personal observations.

This is part of the total marketing review (and SWOT analysis). In terms of promotion, it is primarily concerned to show clearly the interrelationship of customer categories (the type of firm, organisation or individual), products or services and business (new business – a new customer, extension – or an existing customer buying more and so on). It may be necessary to plan different strategies to address specific areas, for example to promote sales to a specific kind of business with which there has been no previous contact.

Once a need has been identified, it must be established that the support planned is likely to be the most cost-effective method of meeting that need. Then the planning stage can commence.

Prepare the operation plan

The first stage of any plan must be to quantify the objectives. A clear, specific statement is needed of what is to be achieved. An objective of improving business is not precise enough, but one of improving the number of new customers buying product A by 20% this year makes it clear to everyone exactly what the goal is and how success will be measured.

Once the objective is finalised, tactics can be selected. This will depend on several factors, including:

▶ The market available

- What is its nature?
- Is it buoyant or is it in a low period?
- Is it price conscious? If so, how?
- What is the competition doing?
- What is the customer profile?

▶ The target audience

- Types of people/organisation?
- What are their buying habits?
- What motivates buyers?
- What are their current attitudes to promotion?

▶ The products or services offered

- What is the current performance?
- What are the strengths and weaknesses?
- What promotional support has been received in the past?
- What production capacity is available?
- Market profile or image?
- Position in life-cycle (is it seen as new and interesting or old and dull)?

▶ Corporate organisation

- What are the current sales and promotional methods?
- Would some tactics cause internal difficulties, for example in terms of administration or resources?
- Is the organisation involved in any other activity that might affect the action intended or detract from it?

Having answered these questions, there may still be other tactics available, all of which could be suitable for achieving the objective. Which tactic to select and use may then depend on which is the most cost-effective. This involves major decisions such as whether to distribute through retail outlets or via the internet.

When the tactics have been decided, the details should be formalised in a written operation plan, even in a small firm. This should not be a one-off exercise, but will eventually provide a reference that can be updated regularly to create the plan for the next period. This "rolling" plan should include:

▶ background information on why the promotional support is necessary;

▶ the objectives;

▶ profile of the target audience(s);

▶ reference to product or service details;

▶ details of additional support other than that actually planned, perhaps that being done by associated offices or various staff;

▶ budget details – how much the action is estimated to cost;

▶ details of how the plan will be implemented;

▶ controls, standards and methods of obtaining results;

▶ an action plan, or timetable, showing what actions are required, who should carry them out, and when.

There are several ways of making the decision on the budget more logical, for example using comparisons with competitors, standard percentages of revenue and so on.

Prepare for implementation

As long as the operational plan has been prepared correctly, the pre-implementation preparation should be a formality. However, this will be the case only if the operational plan has been discussed and agreed with everyone concerned with the support activity and well before any action is required. This means that all the relevant people in the organisation can offer ideas or identify snags. Such consultation can result in (surprisingly) good contributions; it also makes people feel involved and more likely to commit themselves to the next stage.

Implementation

The success or failure of any promotional activity, providing it has been thoroughly planned, then rests on how well it is implemented. Effective implementation depends on how well the details are communicated around the organisation and how implementation is then controlled so that everyone plays their part. Control must also maximise feedback while promotional activity is running to permit any necessary or desirable changes to be made at the earliest opportunity.

Analysis to affect future activity

Any promotional campaign can involve a great deal of people's time and is often expensive in terms of opportunity cost. This is true regardless of what is spent on other aspects of marketing.

It is thus important to know how money is being spent and what is being achieved. Examining the results of every form of promotional activity will show:

▶ What the situation was prior to the activity.

▶ What achievement (the objective) was intended.

▶ What the situation is after the promotional activity has ended (and what has been achieved).

▶ Whether any external factors might have influenced the result, what they were (for example, competitive activity, legislation changes) and their effect.

▶ What has happened to the rest of the market or at least near competitors.

▶ What might have happened if the promotion had not been carried out.

▶ What the budget was and how it was spent.

Careful analysis of what has been achieved is important, not least in planning of what to do next, which must be part of a continuing cycle.

The broader picture

No promotional activity can be carried out in isolation, particularly without linked sales follow-up and service to support it. This activity must be planned too, so as an addendum to the promotional plan there must be a focus on sales activity. Again it should be action oriented, covering the following:

▶ How much prospecting will be done, when, how and by whom?

▶ Who will follow up leads, to what timescale?

▶ What sales targets are required?

▶ What records will be kept?

Planning and implementing a sound, systematic promotional plan is not easy, nor is making sure that all the back-up resources, people, skills and systems are geared to converting the initial enthusiasm created in potential customers into actual business. But such a plan is necessary and, when drawn up and implemented successfully, provides a sound basis for securing and, more importantly, enlarging any business.

Lastly, a promotional plan should contain a section dealing with "other issues", for instance answering more questions such as:

▶ Does a sales initiative (involving formal presentations, perhaps) require training in advance?

▶ Is recruitment needed to add the new skills required in future?

▶ Does the organisation or its structure need changing (for example, new job descriptions)?

▶ Do systems or controls need adjustment?

Every significant activity may need its own plan as a sub-section of the overall plan, and the marketing plan must be linked to the business plan and to specific issues such as management roles, structure and succession, legal matters, research and development, production, quality control and capital equipment, personnel and training activity and information technology.

Business planning (and all its components) is a broad issue. What has been described here is a minimum approach to the marketing element of such a plan, and more may be necessary, especially in large businesses. A sound foundation makes everything to do with marketing more likely to succeed.

There can be advantages in keeping plans for existing products and new ventures separate (while making sure that they operate in an integrated fashion). If that is done, new ventures may justify the addition of further dedicated plans.

Keeping control

Two things are important:

▶ Corrective action. If the results achieved diverge from the plan, the controls need a diagnostic element. It may be necessary to discover why things are going wrong and to fine tune activity so that the deviation is overcome and the revised activity still produces the intended results.

▶ Positive feedback. Just as important is analysis when things are proceeding better than planned. Again questions must be asked and the answers may indicate positive lessons to build into future plans or positive action that should be taken quickly. This point is examined in Chapter 9.

Key points

As Tom Hopkins, a management guru, said:

If you're not planning where you want to be, what reason or excuse do you have for worrying about being nowhere?

To help achieve success a plan must be:

▶ approached systematically;

▶ based on sound, recent information;

▶ practical and able positively to assist the decision-making and action that drive the business.

The process involved in creating a marketing plan must be:

▶ given some time;

▶ formalised – that is, linked to agreed formats, timing and other internal systems;

▶ based on up-to-date data;

▶ analysed (whatever techniques may be used to assist with this);

▶ discussed – getting inputs and ideas from all the appropriate people is part of the process;

▶ finalised and agreed;

▶ documented – the plan must be written down;

▶ communicated – to all those in the organisation who can benefit from knowing the plan and who may be involved in its implementation (a cut down version of the plan may be needed for this);

▶ linked to implementation;

▶ the basis for a rolling plan – one plan becomes a basis for the next.

Co-ordination and control

The ability to learn faster than our competitors
may be our only sustainable competitive weapon.
Arie De Geus, former corporate planning director, Royal Dutch/Shell

Assuming an organisation is sufficiently customer focused and well organised to create marketing plans and implement them, the next consideration is monitoring and controlling what happens. Reality dictates that plans never work out exactly and always need adapting. Indeed, what is ultimately done may depend on what happens along the way. For instance, when Ford or Toyota launch a new saloon, they may add to the range (an estate car, convertible or performance model) if the basic model sells well.

Control in marketing is similar in concept to other forms of management control. It depends upon the comparison of actual (A) performance against pre-set standards (S) and taking corrective action based upon the resulting variances (V) according to the formula:

$$A - S = +/- V$$

The objectives and plans will form the basis of the standards. For instance, the sales plan will contain sales forecasts, which can be translated into targets for each member of the sales team.

It is difficult to assess and control activities which, for the most part, depend upon human reaction and cannot be easily separated from other influences. Consequently, many areas of promotion have been viewed as unmeasurable. Investigating an individual element, such as advertising, and asking how much it will affect sales is an example, because sales do not depend upon advertising alone. But there are exceptions. For instance, responses to direct mail can be tracked accurately, especially if this is the only form of promotion used; so too can visits to a website.

If, however, it is clearly specified what the advertising is supposed to do (perhaps to impress a certain message on a certain number of people of a certain type), it is possible to define standards of performance and evaluate achievement. Control of some form should be exercised in marketing as in other organisational functions. All marketing activities are quantifiable in money terms and thus budgetary control can be exercised.

For marketing activities to be effective the marketing function must be integrated and well co-ordinated with the rest of the company.

Implementing the plan

Successful implementation of a marketing plan depends upon effective management of the five Ws:

▶ What – the goals, objectives and aims.

▶ Who – the people responsible/accountable for realising the plan.

▶ Where – the specific, identified, quantified marketplaces.

▶ When – the period covered by the plan.

▶ Why – the reasons and desired outcomes.

The person wearing the marketing hat must make sure that all material marketing resources are in place, including:

▶ people;

▶ product or service;

▶ internal promotion aids (such as sales aids);

▶ external promotion campaigns (such as advertising);

▶ packaging;

▶ budgetary management systems;

▶ sales data systems;

▶ performance standards.

Once the plan is launched, the focus moves to control.

Maintaining control

The plan should contain specific financial, marketing, sales, distribution and promotion objectives. These provide a basis for performance standards in a number of areas, including product sales (both value and volume) and, where appropriate, in terms of market share.

There are various types of performance standards:

▶ Annual targets express performance expectations in terms of sales, profit and market share. Annual targets are known as absolute targets. Variances will identify what has gone right or wrong, but not why.

▶ Moving standards express the annual targets in divisions of the plan period, that is, monthly or quarterly data with cumulative figures and trends. Again, although moving standards can forecast deviations from the plan, they will not identify why performance differs from the required targets.

▶ Diagnostic standards can identify what is causing the variations and why, and may indicate that additional action is required.

Table 9.1 shows the different elements of control applied to the marketing plan.

Variance analysis

Variances are calculated by comparing actual results with the preset standards. First, cumulative totals are used so that individual monthly variations will tend to cancel each other out. Second, moving annual totals (MATs) can be used by taking 12 months' performance up to and including the month in question. As the most recent month is added and the figure for the same month in the previous year is deducted, the trend will indicate present performance compared with the same period in the previous year.

> **Table 9.1** Elements of control in the marketing plan

Type of control	Objective of control	Standards	How to measure performance	What to look for
Annual product plan control	To examine whether plan objectives are being achieved	Sales quotas and market share financial targets	Comparison of actual results against standards set in each performance area	Notable shortfall between standard and actual Failure of individual sales territories to achieve sales targets by buyer category
Profitability control	To examine whether financial objectives are being met	Profitability by product or product group	Comparison of actual results against standards	Major shift in production mix Spending levels above plan levels Declining sales
Efficiency/ productivity control	To evaluate and improve results of marketing expenditure	Promotional deadlines Distribution targets Sales force activities	Comparison of actual results against advertising plan Sales force: who called on; how many; call frequency; what done in each call	Failure to meet deadlines or set standards in each area of promotion

This enables comparisons to be made on a single diagram of monthly performance against target, cumulative performance against target and, via the moving annual total, the present year versus the previous year.

With good control systems and feedback mechanisms, marketers can quickly identify sales performance variances and the true reasons for them and react to changed circumstances. By monitoring the plan they will be able to report monthly (or whatever time-scale is agreed), and answer the following questions, which may be raised by management:

▶ Are the plan's objectives being met?

▶ What are the variances between budget and actual?

▶ What is causing these variances?

▶ What actions are being taken to correct them?

▶ Is a re-forecast or re-budget necessary?

Marketing never guarantees success but, carefully applied and monitored, it increases the likelihood of achieving it. In a commercial environment, an organisation's success is measured by its profitability.

Measuring corporate financial performance

Marketing must always relate to the planned financial intentions of the organisation. Plans usually specify various targets, which can include profit, sales by revenue and volume, margins and market share as appropriate. A common measure of overall corporate performance used by businesses is return on capital employed (ROCE). This ratio, which measures the return on investment as a percentage, is calculated by expressing net profit as a percentage of capital employed. Capital employed is the amount of long-term money invested in the business and is equivalent to the net assets employed. Table 9.2 overleaf gives some definitions of financial terms. (For more detailed information see *The Economist Guide to Financial Management* by John Tennent.)

The primary ratio of ROCE is a function of two secondary ratios connected by "the multiplier", that is:

$$\text{ROCE} = \frac{\text{net profit}}{\text{capital employed}} \times 100\% = \frac{\text{sales}}{\text{capital employed}} \times \frac{\text{net profit}}{\text{sales}} \times 100\%$$

$$= \text{asset turn} \times \text{ROS}\%$$

▶ If ROS improves, ROCE goes up.

▶ If asset turn improves, ROCE goes up.

▶ If ROS and asset turn improve, ROCE gets the multiplier effect.

> **Table 9.2** Some financial terms defined

Net profit	Also referred to as EBIT (earnings before interest and tax) or operating profit
Capital employed (CE)	The long-term money invested in the company consisting of shareholder's equity (shares plus retained earnings) and long-term loans
Net assets employed (NAE)	Fixed assets plus working capital
Fixed assets	Money tied up in land, buildings, plant and machinery
Working capital	Current assets (excluding cash) minus current liabilities
Current assets	Money tied up in inventory (stock), work in progress, finished goods, receivables (debtors), cash and so on
Current liabilities	Money owed in the short term, for example payables (creditors), overdraft, tax, dividends
Gross profit	Sales revenue minus the cost of goods sold
Gross margin	Gross profit as a percentage of sales
Net margin	Also referred to as return on sales (ROS). Net profit as a percentage of sales
Balance sheet	The overall statement of a company's position at one moment in time, usually the end of the financial year, showing the sources of finance (capital employed) and how it is deployed (net assets employed)
Income statement	A statement showing the results of a company's trading in the period, indicating revenue, expenditure and thus profit or loss (it used to be called the profit and loss account)

To improve ROS:

▶ sales need to increase (through either volume or price) without a proportionate increase in costs;

▶ there is an improvement in sales mix (selling more of better margin products);

▶ costs are reduced.

To improve asset turn:

▶ sales need to increase without a proportionate increase in fixed assets and working capital (remember CE = NAE, see Table 9.2);

▶ investment is reduced (for example, by reducing inventory).

Marketing decisions need to be evaluated in terms of their impact on both sides of the multiplier.

Identifying the profitability input of marketing

A ratio tree (also called a hierarchy or pyramid of ratios) can be constructed to cover total company operations and used to help identify marketing's contribution to ROCE. Marketers will usually recognise their responsibilities in the ROS portion of the ratio tree; this is a natural development from the sales-oriented approach. In this part of the tree, the ratios can be used effectively in analysing the reasons for performance change. It is also illuminating to carry out analysis to identify the relative importance of volume, price, cost and mix changes, particularly in those organisations that believe the solution to every profitability problem is to increase sales volumes.

Some problems are inherent. For example, it is surprising how few sales managers clearly recognise their contributions (inputs) to the asset turn part of the multiplier.

Two major components of working capital are inventory (stock) and receivables (debtors). Although a sales manager may not have direct control over granting credit, debt collection and inventory availability, sales policies must affect them and thus the company's ROCE. Paradoxically, if a sales manager wishes to increase sales volume, two tactics that can be used are immediate ex-inventory delivery and generous credit terms. These will usually increase sales but they could have a disastrous effect on the asset turn part, leading to a lower ROCE.

Marketing must work with other departments to deliver the required levels of profitability on both existing and additional sales. For example:

▶ Who should set inventory (stock) levels?

▶ Who should control credit when it is used as a promotional tool?

▶ Is the product mix sufficiently specified and controlled?

Given that "you get what you measure", performance measures (targets, metrics, key performance indicators or KPIS) must be set carefully. If marketing is measured purely on sales volumes, there can be a lack of focus on mix, costs and investment. Some compromise is necessary between functions: for example, concentrating solely on reducing inventory is dangerous and may lead to inventory shortages or even a period when there is no inventory.

The control element of marketing is evident in many ways. For example, when people buy books from the Amazon website, every time they log on they can see their buying (and search) record being linked to recommendations. In this way, literally mouse click by mouse click, recorded customer information is turned into tactical marketing activity to build the customer relationship and promote new sales. This immediacy is peculiar to e-commerce, but the principle of using past information to prompt action to influence the future is classic.

A final, but fundamental, consideration is cash. Profit and cash flow are not the same. Businesses do not necessarily fail because they make a loss, but they do fail if they run out of cash. All marketing spend is made in the anticipation of enhancing future revenues. Cash flows out on marketing, advertising, new equipment and the building of inventories, and often goods are sold on credit so the business has to wait for any cash to flow in. Cash flow needs to be managed to make sure that there is sufficient funding in place to bridge the working capital gap between paying suppliers and getting paid by customers.

Systematic review

Ultimately, what makes marketing succeed is attention to detail and systematic review of all the important areas and the things that affect them with a view to what action can be taken to maximise effectiveness.

The starting point is to ask questions about economic and political, environmental, social, legislative and technological issues affecting the market. For example, what changes might a looming election suggest? Once that is done, the marketing system must be put under the microscope, asking questions about:

▶ markets;

▶ distribution;

▶ competition;

▶ customer attitudes;

▶ corporate intention;

▶ products and services;

▶ price and pricing policy;

▶ communications tactics (the presentational aspects of the three Ps – product, price, presentation).

A single question, such as asking if the job of the sales team is well defined, might lead to a new focus and a change in sales practices that increases sales. The same is true of every aspect of marketing operations.

Poor control can cause major problems. For example, to shift a surplus of vacuum cleaners, in 1992 Hoover's British division put together one of the most disastrous promotional schemes ever implemented, offering two free return flights to the United States for customers who spent more than £100. Many people did not want a cleaner but bought one just for the flights. So massive was the demand that most people did not get them. Lack of control over how the scheme worked triggered numerous customer complaints and bad media coverage, and cost the company almost £50m in compensation payments. Similarly, failure to monitor

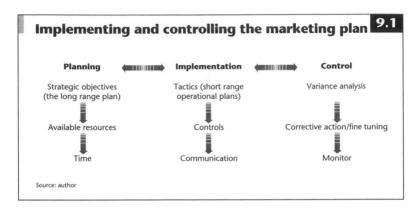

Implementing and controlling the marketing plan 9.1

Planning	⬅️|||⬅️➡️|||➡️	Implementation	⬅️|||⬅️➡️|||➡️	Control
Strategic objectives (the long range plan)		Tactics (short range operational plans)		Variance analysis
⬇		⬇		⬇
Available resources		Controls		Corrective action/fine tuning
⬇		⬇		⬇
Time		Communication		Monitor

Source: author

product use led Unilever to withdraw Persil Power, an extra detergent that consumers could add to regular Persil, which proved so powerful that it damaged clothes. Conversely, careful monitoring of something like advertising might show that a change in the use of media would be beneficial.

Control procedures can answer the crucial question: how will we know when we get there? Not only will they answer it, but they will also allow regular opportunities for fine-tuning performance. Control provides a hand on the tiller to adjust course when things are not going exactly to plan; and, just as important, it makes it possible for organisations to take advantage of changes that present sometimes unexpected opportunities.

Key points

▶ Co-ordination and control are crucial to the marketing process.

▶ The progression from planning to implementation to control in a continuing cycle (see Figure 9.1) is as important overall as any of the individual elements.

▶ Given good factual information, the process can work well and contribute to marketing success.

4

Marketing communications

Influencing buyer behaviour

Advertising isn't a science. It's persuasion. And persuasion is an art.

Leo Burnett, founder, Leo Burnett advertising agency

The third P of the marketing mix is promotion (or presentation). Potential customers must be informed about the product. This involves a variety of communications and techniques, each directed in different ways at different target audiences with the aim of achieving particular objectives. Whatever the mix, the communications strategy must be designed with profitability in mind, although short-term profitability may be deemed less important than longer-term profitability.

At its heart, promotional and sales communication must relate to and use the psychology of how customers assess what is offered to them and make a decision to buy or not, and to buy from one supplier rather than another.

Different types of buyer

Figure 10.1 overleaf illustrates the different types of buyers that marketing communications are aimed at. It shows the marketer starting at the bottom of a pyramid with a mass audience, then progressing towards a decreasing number of customers, some of whom will in effect act as additional unpaid sales people for the product. Many factors will influence whether a suspect converts into a customer and then remains a loyal customer.

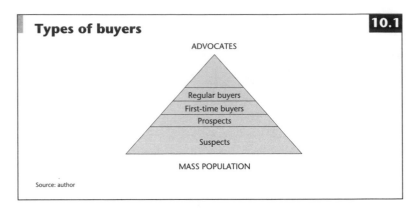

Types of buyers **10.1**

ADVOCATES

Regular buyers
First-time buyers
Prospects

Suspects

MASS POPULATION

Source: author

The types of people in these categories are as follows:

▶ Suspects. Those that the marketer believes could be interested in the product on offer, but who, in the case of an existing product, have not previously enquired about it or bought it.

▶ Prospects (identifying target audiences). Those who have not yet bought, but who have indicated an "interest", perhaps in response to an advertisement. Prospects may be gathering information from several sources to help them make a choice, and they may be ready to buy now or sometime in the future. Either way, how marketers then react to this interest may make the difference between purchase and no purchase.

▶ First-time buyers/customers (converting enquiries into sales). Customers who have made their first purchase could become loyal long-term customers. This will depend on the customers' experience of the product and how the organisation develops its relationship with them.

▶ Repeat buyers/customers (winning repeat orders). Customers who have made more than one purchase become long-term buyers. Whether they do so will depend on, for example:

– Long time spans between purchases, for example buying a new mobile telephone. A customer may be loyal to a particular brand, but may not choose to trade in the old model for some time. One reason manufacturers constantly change and improve their products is to shorten that time span. The same is true about cars, but over a longer timescale.

- The relationship between the customer and the organisation. If a positive relationship is developing, the customer may purchase more. For example, people may choose to fly with the same airline or take a holiday with the same cruise company because they like the product (the flight and the cruise) and the staff (the service). The same is true of Apple, whose loyal customers will not use any other brand of computer.
- The opportunity for constant repeat purchases, for example Heinz beans. However, other factors including quality of the product, pricing and packaging affect the purchasing decisions.

▶ Advocates (helping to build brand loyalty over time). These are the ultra-desirable customers who are loyal to the product/brand and who act as evangelists for it by recommending it. Again, Apple is a good example.

Making buying decisions

Marketers must design approaches based on the fact that a buyer's decision-making process goes through a logical series of steps in order to make a final decision:

▶ Recognising a need. For example, a person may develop a headache while out shopping and seek to remedy the discomfort as soon as possible by purchasing a painkiller.

▶ The level of "involvement". The customer determines how much time and effort to invest in satisfying a need. Continuing the example, the customer will probably want to find a quick headache remedy and will therefore spend little time making a decision (in the jargon, the "involvement").

▶ Identifying alternatives. The customer considers the various alternatives available, probably noting that there are several types of analgesic available – aspirin, paracetamol, ibupofren and more. These are available through either well-known branded names or the own-label brands of chains.

▶ Evaluation. The customer analyses the advantages and

disadvantages of the alternatives identified, perhaps the strengths available, any possible side-effects, whether they are in tablet or capsule form, the number of doses in a pack and the price. Consideration includes taking a view of the image and reputation of a brand. In this instance, all this may take only a moment, though for other purchases it may take considerable time.

▶ Purchasing decision. The customer decides what to purchase.

▶ Post-purchase behaviour. The customer seeks reassurance that the purchasing decision was correct. How quickly the headache goes away will affect future purchasing decisions.

People will buy a headache pill when necessary, but many decisions take into account other priorities. Thus a decision to buy a new suit or go out for a meal will be balanced against other, perhaps more necessary purchases.

Given the purchasing power that exists, certainly in the developed world, as much marketing is directed at less necessary goods as it is at more essential products; perhaps more. An example is the goods that are displayed alongside supermarket checkouts which are there partly because customers decide about such purchases quickly. They sell from that position because marketers recognise the psychological reasons for making buying decisions.

Consumers use a variety of criteria to compare and contrast different alternatives. Some of the things that will influence their decisions are shown in Table 10.1.

The design of a popular novel's cover illustrates the principles set out above. Past experience is evoked by comparisons with other titles and reminders of an author's previous work. The term "bestseller" hints at large numbers of satisfied customers, and references to advertising or programme tie-ins – "as seen on TV" – aim to add credibility, as do quotes from reviews from an authoritative source. All these marketing features take account of the way people buy.

The whole look is important; so too are other factors. For example, a book may appear first as a hardback (and at what some customers might see as a high price) then later as a paperback, targeting a larger market. It may also be sold through specialist outlets such

Table 10.1 Examples of buying criteria

Criterion	Influencing factors
Past experience of particular brands	Consumers may have used a particular branded product in the past and believe that it was more effective than others, even though it may contain the same ingredients as other brands; similarly, consumers will turn against branded products they have not deemed satisfactory
Experience of friends and family	Word-of-mouth recommendations are extremely powerful in influencing purchasing decisions
Advertising and marketing	Advertising and promotional campaigns can be powerful in influencing purchasing decisions and brand image
Specialist advice	Many consumers lack confidence or are ignorant about the attributes of particular products and seek specialist advice to inform their purchasing decision from a pharmacist or wine merchant, for example

as book clubs, where either a special price or the need to maintain commitments to the club may prompt purchases. Even the time of year at which a book is published can be used: many books are published before Christmas in the belief (or hope) that they will be bought as presents; and titles thought attractive for holiday reading come out in paperback early in the summer.

What influences buyers' decisions

When their evaluation of the alternatives is complete, consumers have to decide whether to purchase or not. A decision not to purchase may be only temporary until other alternatives become available.

In a retail context, someone's decision to buy at a particular store may be based on a variety of influences, such as:

▶ the level of helpfulness, knowledge and courtesy of staff;

▶ the layout of the store and the display and range of products on show;

> **Table 10.2** Categories of buyer behaviour

Category	Description
People	People are influenced in many ways by a variety of different people. They may be friends, family, heroes (for example, football players or pop stars), teachers, co-workers and more
Culture	Cultural influences come from nationality, religion, class and the circles we mix in
Lifestyle	People may purchase products that reflect the reality of their lives, or they may be aspirational, making at least some purchasing decisions according to the lifestyle they would like to lead, which would almost certainly involve spending more than they would if their purchasing was grounded in reality. This can include buying into new product areas
Financial	Poor people (unless tempted by easy credit) will be extremely price sensitive and focus on purchasing basic products, whereas rich people can afford to buy a wider range of products or services. That does not mean, however, that in their own way they will be any less price sensitive
Media	The media have great influence over what people buy. This can range from reviews of films, plays and books (which may be either positive or negative) through to healthy eating campaigns. Negative publicity can kill a product – positive publicity is a very potent force in influencing sales
Necessities	People must buy life's necessities. Food and housing at the very least; necessities are closely linked to financial circumstances or may be distress purchases – fixing a broken car, for example
Health concerns	Changed risks prompt changed purchase patterns such as special socks bought by airline passengers after all the publicity about deep vein thrombosis (DVT). The same is true of ecological and environmental factors
Fashion	So much is bought in the name of fashion, as the phrase "fashion victim" suggests

▶ discounts and sales offers – price is always important;

▶ additional charges – for example, whether delivery is an extra cost or free;

▶ methods of payment – for example, the incentive to make interest-free payments over six months or a year or even to delay any payment for a year.

There are many disparate influences on purchasing behaviour. Those outlined in Table 10.2 indicate how complex that behaviour can be.

Some influences fall outside the above categories, for example those of the government, the weather, alcohol (people are more likely to buy when relaxed) and word of mouth.

Influencing people to make purchases

Public relations, advertising, direct mail, sales promotion and many other techniques are among the ways of changing attitudes and moving customers towards making a purchase.

Objectives en route to purchase

Transitional objectives that may persuade consumers to buy include:

▶ getting them to try a product;

▶ getting them to buy more or buy more frequently;

▶ extending the use of the product, thus getting them to buy more – for example, Kellogg's breakfast cereal is promoted as an evening snack;

▶ instilling trust in a brand so that new products under the brand name are also bought – for example, Mars was able to extend its brand appeal from chocolate bars to ice cream and drinks;

▶ associating with a product through merchandising spin-offs – for example, Lego developed model kits based on *Star Wars* film characters.

Building customer awareness

The sequence of the customer moving from being unaware of an organisation or product to being a regular user provides a framework for considering promotional activity. Each of the six steps described below represents a change in attitude.

1 Unawareness to awareness

▶ At this stage prospective customers move from no knowledge of a product to where they know about it, or at least of its existence. Their attitude is receptive but passive and their major need is information. Promotion is targeted at:

▶ introducing a concept;

▶ telling the prospect that something more specific exists;

▶ creating an automatic association between the needs of the organisation and the customers.

2 Awareness to interest

This is a move from a passive state to an active one. Interest is aroused by the product's newness, appearance, or something that is said about it. The response can be active or passive. Promotional objectives here are to:

▶ gain customers' attention through the message;

▶ create interest in the product;

▶ provide a succinct summary of all the relevant information in the prospect's mind.

At this stage all the aspects of the promotion mix begin to get people to say "I must check this product out".

3 Interest to evaluation

Potential buyers will first consider the effect of the product in a variety of ways, including its image, qualities and functions, lifestyle, circumstances and needs. They will analyse the pros and cons and look for what suits them; they may also look for more information, something to confirm their initial impressions. Because interested people are not that far from making a decision, selling attempts can be made to:

▶ create a situation that encourages them to start this phase of reasoning;

▶ discover and focus on their relevant wants and needs;

▶ segment and target buyers according to their requirements.

4 Evaluation to trial

People will want to try the product and evaluate its suitability. Promotional objectives here are to:

▶ clearly identify the usage opportunities;

▶ suggest a timescale for trial – this could be a few moments for evaluating a fragrance or trying clothing to a day or more to test drive a car or assess sporting equipment.

The intention is to encourage first purchase and get people to say "this looks good and does all I require, I'll buy it".

5 Trial to purchase

The buyer will take this step if the trial has been successful. The objectives of promotion are to:

▶ provide reminders of such things as brand, image or technical advantages;

▶ emphasise success and satisfaction;

▶ remind people of other usage opportunities and provide supporting proof via third-party references.

6 Purchase to repeat purchase

This is the final objective of the promotion and, while buyers may well assess other suppliers, when people move from occasional usage to constant usage, this selection of the product will be become largely automatic – until something happens to upset the status quo. The objectives are now simpler, though not necessarily easier to achieve, and are to:

▶ maintain the climate that has led to satisfaction;

▶ keep up the image;

▶ maintain contact and confirm the essential qualities of the product and advise of other associated products.

Beyond this sequence, buyers, having perhaps changed from a product they have used for many years, may feel that they must try several other products, not just one, now their buying pattern has changed. This is what promotion must influence.

Making promotion work

The promotional mix of the elements that have influenced the customer along the way can be many and varied, from something small such as a leaflet through the door to a major advertising poster campaign on hoardings. With this in mind, marketing can utilise and deploy the individual techniques, making them all work together to achieve exactly what is wanted. The impact of each technique will be different and it may be difficult to determine which technique has had what impact. People's image of an organisation and its products is the cumulative effect of everything they see and hear about it.

Different advertisements address different stages in this process. For example, most advertising for a brand such as Coca-Cola is to keep past customers buying Coke rather than something else, though it may also include an appeal to potential new customers.

Importantly, promotion can only work, especially in the long term, when what is done is acceptable to customers. In part, confidence and certainty come from the knowledge people have of suppliers. One reason branding works is that buyers regard brands as some sort of guarantee. As Russell Hanlin, CEO of Sunkist Growers, says:

An orange is an orange ... is an orange. Unless that orange happens to be Sunkist, a name 80% of consumers know and trust.

If purchasers have problems with a product or brand they will not come back for more. Sometimes promotion succeeds in selling products that are substandard, or even illegal or dangerous, something no respectable marketer would condone. In many countries legislation controls such matters. Other sanctions exist too – advertising, for instance, is regulated primarily through a voluntary code of practice. If something is inappropriate (such as racist) or simply untruthful, advertisers can be made to stop a campaign in circumstances that probably guarantee bad publicity. This acts to control most excesses. Some campaigns push the limits. For example, some see fashion chain French Connection UK's logo "FCUK" as inappropriate, but it is used to promote the brand globally. Sometimes, however, being on the borderline can be effective marketing, and certainly where the borderline is changes as attitudes change. Some organisations make their attitude to fair play clear as part of their intended appeal to consumers; Levi Strauss publicises its approval of the International Labour Organisation standards to counter stories of clothes made by sweat-shop labour in developing countries.

Key points

Understanding buyer behaviour leads to precise promotion. Marketers must:

▶ be aware of the individuality of their customers and potential customers;

▶ understand how customers approach making a buying decision and the many reasons that prompt them to act;

▶ relate this information to the market and style of product (and its potential consumer);

▶ act to implement promotional activity in a way that is designed to work with reality, not simply to be strident about their offering in a vacuum.

If promotional activity, whatever it may be – an advertisement, a brochure, a website – is based on this, even if it still needs to be creatively executed, it stands a much better chance of being effective than would otherwise be the case.

Marketing communications: the detail

There is no such thing as "soft sell" and "hard sell". There is only "smart sell" and "stupid sell".

Charles Bowder, former president, BBDO

Marketing communications can take many forms: press and public relations, advertising, direct mail promotion, sales promotion, merchandising and display, leaflets, websites and so on. More unusual but increasingly popular are the following:

▶ Viral marketing – for example, Lee Jeans emailing film clips to attract people to a website that is then linked to advertising.

▶ Product placement – various manufacturers have paid to have their products featured in films and television programmes, for example Omega, BMW and Ericsson in James Bond movies.

▶ Sponsorship – Dame Ellen MacArthur was helped in her round-the-world sailing success by Kingfisher's sponsorship over five years; Tiger Woods has long been associated with Nike; Manchester United (an international business as well as a football club) uses sponsorships extensively, for a long time working with AIG (though in volatile economic times any sponsor quoted may change).

▶ Ads in odd places – if they are odd enough, their very presence can generate more coverage; even the space shuttle has carried advertisements.

Marketers must decide the "best" mix and how much money to spend on different elements of it. Whatever they do, it must be creatively deployed and always cost-effective, although it is not always easy to work out what the effect of a particular method has been.

What is promotion?

Promotion encompasses everything to do with the way an organisation communicates persuasively with people to influence them towards making a purchase. This may be direct – one mail shot that prompts a reply, which is an order. Or it may be much less direct, involving many stages and influences.

This is sometimes seen as the most interesting part of marketing; certainly it is the most visible, with elements of it – advertisements, posters and so on – all around. It is also an important element. As Ed Johnson (whose quotation appears in the introduction to this book) says:

> They say if you build a better mousetrap than your neighbour, people are going to come running. They are like hell! It's marketing that makes the difference.

Even the producer of the best product or service will do no business if no one knows it exists.

Promotion must be more than passing on information; it must be persuasive and it must differentiate. Potential customers may see the range of goods offered by competitors as being somewhat similar. This is true of many areas, for example cars, with many similar models existing in each category, or copying machines or computers. To a large extent it is the promotional elements that allow people to make a judgment about what is right for them in any product area; this is as true of industrial goods as of consumer goods.

The promotional mix

Mix is the right word for the techniques. Furthermore, in some cases the product itself acts promotionally, with the cover design of a book being important at every level of sale and display, for instance; the packaging is effectively part of the product. Beyond

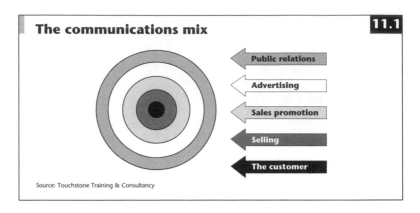

The communications mix

11.1

- Public relations
- Advertising
- Sales promotion
- Selling
- The customer

Source: Touchstone Training & Consultancy

that, the various promotional techniques themselves are not mutually exclusive. They are often used together or in various combinations – different mixes, with one or more technique perhaps predominating. Each works in a rather different way, principally in how directly and in what way it relates to the market. Figure 11.1 shows the distances at which each technique operates from the potential customer (who is at the centre of the target); it is this that characterises the different role that different techniques play.

Promotion does not act in a vacuum: it must relate to the way potential purchasers move progressively towards purchase and influence the attitudes of the target audience. With many products the aim is not just purchase, but repeat purchase, as when a householder restocks with, say, the same brand of soap. The same principle applies to books, for example, persuading:

▶ a college to recommend a book for use on a course;

▶ a reader to buy more of a particular author, series or category of book;

▶ someone to buy more books (of whatever sort) as presents;

▶ people to purchase sequels (this applies to fiction and non-fiction);

▶ people to favour, and trust, a publisher or imprint, prompting the way in which some people will return to the same series of, say, guidebooks.

The buying process

The stages in the buying process were described in Chapter 10. The promotional elements creating the progression to buying can be used in any combination to make up the overall mix: everything from a small detail (such as a review quote on a book cover) to a major campaign (posters on station platforms). The individual effect each promotional element has may be difficult to quantify, but everything people see and hear about an organisation will affect their image of it.

Public relations

Public relations (PR) is concerned primarily with an organisation or brand's overall image. In seeking to create (and then maintain and develop) an image, it helps if marketers have a clear idea of how people perceive the organisation. This can be ascertained through research, and some information can be obtained simply by "keeping an ear to the ground", although people will often say what they think is expected, thus confirming an existing view or prejudice.

The effect of public relations is cumulative so a host of factors, such as the quality of business cards and letterheads, of switchboard and reception, of all printed promotion, of staff appearance and helpfulness, will contribute to an organisation's overall image.

The reason that an organisation may have a strong and positive image will be to a significant extent because of what it tells people about itself. Large companies spend large amounts of money on their corporate image or their brands' images because image always matters – everything from logos to advertising. But image must be backed by substance; a change of logo or name introduced by a new chief executive changes nothing on its own. Companies can also get things wrong, as British Airways did when it removed the national flag from its livery in favour of a variety of bright ethnic designs. The change was much criticised, most notably by Margaret Thatcher, the prime minister at the time. Eventually BA reversed the initiative.

Focus on different target audiences

Public relations should involve a planned and sustained attempt to promote understanding between an organisation and its audiences and a positive interest in the organisation that whets appetites for more information, prompts enquiries, re-establishes dormant contacts, reinforces and enhances its image with its stakeholders, and encourages loyalty to the organisation and its products or services. A company's stakeholders include:

▶ customers and potential customers;

▶ regulatory authorities (for instance, in industries such as finance and pharmaceuticals);

▶ shareholders (especially if the company is involved in structural change or a takeover);

▶ suppliers (who are more likely to put themselves out for a well-respected company);

▶ institutional and other investors;

▶ the wider community, including environmental and other pressure groups (who will be concerned that policies or practices are ethical).

Some PR campaigns are short, focusing on a single theme, brand or product – for instance for an event – and some will seek to reinforce the corporate or brand image in various ways over a long period – for instance for a corporate entity. The audiences sought to be reached may be many and several different campaigns may run in tandem in order to reach them.

Activity that generates good publicity is a powerful weapon in the promotional armoury, although it may not drive sales in the way that is hoped – a series of good reviews rarely make a book a bestseller, though they should help to make it profitable. And the costs of obtaining good publicity are usually less than the costs of advertising. But PR can make large demands on human resources, so in many smaller companies it may be neglected because people are overstretched and thus opportunities are missed. In the end, the effect of a lack of attention to PR will depend on the nature of the business. The makers of electrical goods need good publicity for their products, whereas retailers of electrical goods will rely more on advertising, although they will also want good rather than bad publicity.

So many people affect image

Public relations activity will succeed only if there is a good story to tell, which will depend on a wide range of people in an organisation and its standards of service. In an award-winning training film, *Who Killed the Sale?*, a salesman is shown trying, unsuccessfully, to get an order for an engineering product. Progressively, the potential customer is exposed to others in the organisation and, cumulatively, such a poor image builds up that he is unwilling to place a new order – much to the salesman's bemusement. The salesman's efforts are undermined as follows:

▶ A previous order is wrongly delivered, and the dispatch department, already at fault, makes matters worse by the way in which it attempts to sort it out.

▶ The switchboard operator contributes to an important message for the customer going astray when he visits the factory, as does a harassed girl in the sales office who fails to track him down.

▶ A demonstration is unconvincingly conducted by a technician who fails to realise its importance because he, in turn, was poorly briefed.

▶ The customer overhears a conversation between two more technical people who are dismissive about their own company's engineering competence.

▶ Lastly, as the customer drives away from the factory he is held up and made to reverse by a rude driver who reveals, when he closes it, that his truck door has the company's name on it.

It takes few such incidents to negate the time and money spent on PR, which may have been done in-house or contracted out to a PR firm, often at great expense. Whatever is done, every aspect of corporate reputation is fragile; it is said that any organisation is as good as its last success.

Media relations

Cultivating good relations with the media and taking care over press releases is important in creating the desired corporate image, in managing news about an organisation, especially bad news, and in drawing attention to new products. A campaign of press contact aims to create continuity over and above an individual news item. The impact of what is done is cumulative; customers are made to feel that they regularly see things about an organisation, but sometimes have difficulty remembering the exact context of what was said or, more likely, written. To achieve this cumulative impact, PR people need to be constantly on the lookout for opportunities of gaining a mention.

Even routine matters, such as the appointment of a new member of staff or an office move, may be written up and can contribute to the whole process. This applies particularly to the trade press covering specific areas or industries. Much of the content may be made up of what is often inconsequential news, but it helps to keep a name visible. Some routine stories will get a mention, particularly if the company is well known, but news means just what it says and it will not be published unless the media feel it is useful. Press releases should also be constructed in a way that will grab people's attention. Newspapers, magazines and broadcasters receive thousands of press releases, most of which go straight into the bin after a cursory glance.

If an organisation, or its spokesperson, becomes known as a source of good comment, stories and articles, media contacts will start to come to the person concerned and continue to do so. This helps keep the organisation in the public eye as a trusted "authority". Events can be linked to press and public relations activity. For example, launch parties and premiere activities for new movies.

Advertising

Memorable advertising slogans such as "Just do it" (Nike), Audi's "Vorsprung durch technik" (progress through technology) or "We try harder" (Avis car rental) are hugely effective in promoting a brand. Advertising can be defined as any paid form of non-personal communication directed at target audiences through various media in order to present and promote products, services and ideas. More simply, it is "non-personal salesmanship".

The role of advertising

With some exceptions, as in the case of a product recall, the role of advertising, as one of a number of variable elements in the communications mix, is to boost sales in a cost-effective way. There are many different forms of advertising, each reflecting the role they need to play among the other marketing techniques employed. The targets to which advertising is directed are also varied. They include:

▶ national (or international) advertising;

▶ local advertising;

▶ advertising on websites (a growth area);

▶ direct mail advertising (and leaflets inserted in magazines);

▶ advertising to obtain leads for sales staff;

▶ trade advertising (to those who will resell the product);

▶ sector advertising (for instance, pens may be promoted to the business gifts market separately from their promotion to the retail trade).

Among the many objectives that can be achieved through using advertising in particular ways are the following:

▶ informing potential customers of a new offering;

▶ increasing the frequency of purchase;

▶ increasing the use of a product;

▶ increasing the quantity purchased;

▶ increasing the frequency of replacement;

▶ lengthening any buying seasons;

▶ presenting a promotional programme;

▶ bringing a family of products together;

▶ turning a disadvantage into an advantage;

▶ attracting a new group or generation of customers;

▶ supporting or influencing a retailer, dealer, agent or intermediary;

▶ reducing substitution by maintaining customer loyalty;

▶ making the organisation behind the range of offerings known (corporate image advertising);

▶ stimulating enquiries (from customers and intermediaries);

▶ giving reasons why intermediaries should stock or promote a product;

▶ providing "technical" information.

These are not mutually exclusive and may also link to the product life-cycle (see Chapter 3). However, the main tasks are usually to:

▶ gain customers' attention;

▶ attract customer interest;

▶ create desire for what is offered;

▶ prompt the customer to buy (within a short time or in the more distant future).

Advertising is, therefore, primarily concerned with attitudes and attitude change, specifically creating and sustaining favourable attitudes towards a product.

Fundamentally, however, advertising aims to sell. Every advertisement should relate to the product or service, its market and potential market, and as a piece of communication each can perform a variety of tasks. Thus an advertisement may:

▶ provide information to remind current users or inform non-users of a product's existence;

▶ attempt to persuade current users to purchase again, non-users to buy for the first time and potential new users to change habits or suppliers;

▶ create uncertainty about the ability of current suppliers to best satisfy customers' needs – in this way, advertising can effectively persuade potential customers to try an alternative product or brand (extreme versions of this are referred to as "knocking copy", used sometimes by, among others, car manufacturers, which are openly critical of competitors);

▶ reinforce the idea that current purchases satisfy the customer's needs well – this maintains awareness and aims to prompt continuing purchases;

▶ reduce the uncertainty felt by customers immediately following an important purchase, as they think about whether or not they have made the correct choice.

Types of advertising

There are four basic types of advertising:

▶ Primary – to stimulate basic demand for a particular type of product, such as insurance or coffee.

▶ Selective – to promote an individual brand name, for a toilet soap or toothpaste, for example, which may be promoted without particular reference to the manufacturer's identity.

▶ Product – to promote a product or range of related brands where some account must be taken of the image and interrelationship of products in the mix.

▶ Institutional – to promote an organisation's name, image and services.

Advertising media and methods

A great variety of advertising media are available and a mix must be selected that fits the purpose of both the organisation and the product. Among the main categories are:

▶ Newspapers, which often enjoy reader loyalty and, hence, high credibility. Consequently, they are particularly useful for prestige and reminder advertising, especially as readers often spend more time looking through Saturday and Sunday editions. Local newspapers are obviously useful for anything local and they are sometimes used to test market area advertising support before a national launch.

▶ Colour supplements (accompanying such papers) are ideal for general advertising, but they appeal to a relatively limited part of the readership and often charge premium rates.

▶ Magazines vary from quarterlies to weeklies and from general, wide-coverage journals to those with a specific focus, such as trade magazines, or linked to highly specialised interests. Similarly, different magazines of the same type (such as women's magazines) appeal to different age and socio-economic groups. Magazines are often read on a regular basis.

▶ Television is regarded as the best overall medium for achieving a mass impact and creating an immediate or quick sales response. It is arguable whether or not the audience is captive or receptive, but the fact that television is being used is often sufficient in itself to generate trade support. Television allows the product to be shown or demonstrated and is useful in test marketing new consumer products because of its regional nature, but it is expensive and therefore ruled out for almost anything except mass-market products.

▶ Outdoor advertising is useful in a support role in a campaign through, for example, strategically placed posters near to busy thoroughfares or in train stations.

▶ Cinema, with its escapist atmosphere, can have an enormous impact on its audience. But without repetition (people visiting the cinema regularly, or a tie-in with other media) it has little lasting effect. It is useful for backing press and TV advertising, but for certain products only (for example, the BBC has run a campaign to augment other activities, especially on its own channel), bearing in mind the audience and the atmosphere. This is another medium where the cost is high, though it is possible for local businesses to advertise in a single cinema, which is cost-effective.

▶ Commercial radio, playing music for every conceivable taste or focusing on interest groups (news or phone-in fans, or whatever), offers repetitive contact, has proved an excellent outlet for certain products and is expanding its users all the time. For instance, it is used widely to advertise cars and associated motoring products such as windscreen replacement services to drivers who listen to their car radios. Many local radio stations appeal to a wide cross-section of people and thus offer potential support to products ranging from opticians to retailers and, perhaps surprisingly, government.

▶ Websites in recent years have become a significant new medium for advertising, ranging from panels rather like an advertisement on a magazine page to the pop-ups that link with cues given by the use of the site. Some are general, others specialised; indeed almost any minority can be found represented on the web. Google leads the way: eMarketer, an online research agency, reports that in 2006 Google earned 25% of the $14 billion spent on web advertising; it predicts that the value of web advertising will increase and that it will account for a higher proportion of the overall advertising spend. (See also Electronic media, page 175.)

▶ Direct mail (see page 163).

Decisions, not only about different methods, but also about which medium (or media) to use – one newspaper rather than another and so on – can be difficult. Advertising agencies that handle the larger advertising budgets have sophisticated media buying departments to assist in planning the advertising strategy and campaign.

Trade advertising

Not all advertising is aimed at potential consumers; some is directed at distributors and retailers who must be influenced to stock and promote a product.

Even though the sales force often has a prime role to play in achieving stocking and promotional objectives, trade advertising is also important in this respect. Indeed, trade advertising sets the scene for personal sales visits, since it can:

▶ remind intermediaries about the product between sales visits;

▶ keep them informed about developments and changes of policy;

▶ set the scene, so that when potential customers are approached by sales staff they already have some awareness, and perhaps understanding, of the product; this in turn can affect the approach sales people take.

One important aspect of trade advertising is not so much what it says but that it is there. The commitment (and cost) of taking such space is seen as a commitment to particular products. If a sales person is pressing a retailer to take good stocks, instigate promotion or generally take a product seriously, buyers are apt to ask: "What are you doing for it?" This is reasonable: it will be easier to sell a product to intermediaries if the supplier is seen to be taking action to make people want to buy it.

Thus trade advertising often occurs before consumer advertising campaigns to help encourage the ordering of stock in anticipation of future demand to be created by the consumer advertising that will follow. Incentives to order stock are often linked to the trade advertising. For example, when new products are launched or special promotions are introduced, special deals (such as an incentive if a minimum quantity is ordered) or higher (introductory) discounts may be offered to the trade, all of which the trade-targeted advertising can emphasise as well as flagging the timing and weight of any consumer advertising or other promotional support that is scheduled.

Different products demand different approaches; for example, a consumer product may have far more advertising (and other marketing effort) directed at the trade as it is launched when there is a need to persuade stores to stock it. Trade advertising of an established product that sells well will be less necessary as stores will want to reorder it. The level of trade advertising will be heightened to emphasise a product improvement and reduced when all is going well. There is also a link with how technical the product is. Additional efforts may be required to brief or train those who stock a product to be able to explain, perhaps demonstrate, and sell it to their customers, whether they be individuals or businesses.

Advertising strategy

Decisions on the advertising strategy, campaign and choice of media need to be based on an analysis of the market. Research will rarely produce all the facts and may be misinterpreted, but it should be helpful and reduce the chances of failure. However, this is not to say that advertising based on intuition or gut feeling rather than facts will not work. Sometimes it does so extremely well; indeed, many slogans that have become famous may reflect an image suggested by research but the actual writing of them is more a "creative hunch". Once voted people's all-time favourite, the Heinz Baked Beans slogan "Beans mean Heinz" is reputed to have been dreamed up in a pub. Avis's "We try harder" was more clearly based on research showing that they were number two in the market.

Spelling out what needs to be done in a simple document may help, too. This can consist of three succinct paragraphs, describing:

▶ the basic proposition – the promise to the customer and the statement of benefit;

▶ the "reason why" – the support proof justifying the proposition, the main purpose of which is to render the message as convincing as possible;

▶ the "tone of voice" – the manner in which the message should be delivered, the image to be projected and, not infrequently, the picture customers have of themselves, which it could be unwise to disturb or, rather, wise to capitalise on.

Most marketers, when faced with a rough visual and copy lay-out, have an automatic subjective response: they like it or they do not like it. Although the creator may attempt to explain that the appraiser is not a member of the target audience, it can be difficult to be objective. Nevertheless, while an attempt at objectivity must be made, there are few experienced advertising or marketing executives who can say that their judgment has never failed. As Lord Leverhulme of Lever Brothers (now part of Unilever) reputedly once said: "I know that half my advertising budget is wasted, but I'm not sure which half." (A similar remark is also attributed to John Wanamaker, the "father" of modern advertising.)

Another possible problem in any business is that of slavish copying. Advertising gets into a rut; those producing it reiterate an established formula and cease to think creatively. This gives rise to so-called tombstone-style, unillustrated and wordy advertisements, such as those used by the Bank of England when issuing gilt-edged stocks because of the legal requirement to advertise them. They may be cheap and easy to produce, but they are uninspired and unlikely to have real impact.

It is one thing for advertising to be visible but it is quite another for it to be persuasive. There is also a danger of confusing creativity – the process that makes something both appropriate to customers and memorable – with cleverness. Sometimes a clever idea – a play on words in a headline, perhaps – acts not to increase the power of the advertisement but to obscure what should be a clear message.

Every organisation must pose straight questions about its advertising and also about particular advertisements:

▶ Does the advertisement match the strategy laid down?

▶ Does it gain attention and create awareness?

▶ Is it likely to create interest and understanding of the advantages of what it offers?

▶ Does it create a desire for the benefits and really prompt the need to buy?

▶ Is it likely to prompt potential customers to make a purchase, now or in the future?

▶ Can it be linked to tangible action (with a coupon to be completed and returned or a "hotline" to be telephoned, for instance)?

Overall, does the advertising communicate? Will people notice it, understand it, believe it, remember it and buy as a result of it?

The next question is how to make an advertisement effective. There are many ways, such as humour, personalities (the Marlboro cowboy or the Jolly Green Giant), exotic locations, cartoons, even a series of running advertisements, each ending with a cliff-hanger to encourage viewing the next episode. Nestlé was the first to use this, on television in the UK, for Nescafé Gold Blend coffee and even ran press advertisements stating no more than the time and date of the next instalment. It is an example that illustrates that new ideas can still be found, and sales can rise as a result.

Often advertising's task is to make something routine, or even potentially dull, seem interestingly different. Sometimes the product really is interestingly different; more often its essential qualities need presenting in whatever way allows the presentation to persuade. There are many ways of doing this, ranging from advertisements with one catchphrase to others setting out various elements of a product or, if it is essentially similar to competing products, focusing on one – maybe peripheral – aspect to make it seem special. For example, a car rental firm might emphasise that it will deliver to and collect from customers.

The possibilities are endless and the ultimate goal is always to make a product appear different and attractive and therefore desirable.

Advertising also has to look attractive. Sometimes this may be achieved through added humour, personalities and so on, or through lavish production values, which may be costly, but may be worth it if they create something outstanding. But there is a danger that the enhancements hide the message; viewers of a poster or a television advertisement may laugh at its humour yet will not recall the brand being advertised.

Exhibitions

A technique used regularly in some product areas is taking part in exhibitions. Exhibitions (and trade fairs and the like) can be hard work and costly, but they are a useful way of drawing attention to and selling a company's products. The associated advertising needs to attract people to the exhibition; the design of the stand needs to create the appropriate impact once inside; and the people "on duty" need to play their part well. For example, nothing switches visitors off quicker than the stereotyped "can I help you?" to which the reply is usually "no thank you, I'm just looking". Not only does the personal input on the day have to be good; so too does follow-up contact, which must be prompt and appropriate.

Direct mail promotion

Direct mail and electronic direct mail (see page 175) can be an effective promotional and advertising medium. It is often described as "junk mail" because most of it is discarded almost immediately, even unopened, as a result of being poorly targeted. What matters is the sales return judged against the cost of a campaign. With some specialised uses and with mailings to existing customers or those who have signed up to receive the mailing, as in the cases of some clothing firms and centres of the performing arts, the quantity sent may be modest but response rates of 50% have been achieved. However, with mass mailing even the more common 1% response can be profitable. The use of direct mail is widespread and is especially prominent in business-to-business marketing and marketing by charities. For firms such as Lands' End and Reader's Digest it is their main form of promotion.

What matters is that direct mail produces sufficient profitable results and does not damage brand image. It is also crucial that the level of customer relations management matches or exceeds the customer's expectations. If it does not, sales will be lost and the opportunities for repeat business will disappear (see Chapter 12).

In the UK, the Post Office, which spends a great deal of time and money studying the effectiveness of direct mail (which is a large part of its business), commissioned independent research which showed that more than 90% of direct mail is opened and more than 75% of it is at least skimmed. As with all promotional and advertising activity, if it is to be successful direct mail must stand out, generate interest and be persuasive.

Direct mail is not an alternative to advertising; it is simply one of the techniques that can be used in the promotional mix. It is no more a magic formula than any other technique. But it can sometimes suit well. It is certainly more flexible than advertising. Direct mail may constitute four letters, or 40, 400, 4,000 or 400,000. It does not have to be used on a grand scale: it can be targeted at small groups or undertaken progressively, with mail shots sent out weekly or monthly. It is personal and can be directed at specific and discrete groups.

It is also controllable, it can be tested and implemented progressively, and its results can be monitored to make sure it provides a cost-effective element in the promotional mix. The cost per contact is comparatively low, and the flexibility of how a campaign is conducted is high. It can be directed specifically, as part of the promotion of particular products, or broadly to sell an organisation.

The elements of direct mail

For direct mail to be successful, attention must be paid to the following:

▶ The list. Any mailing is only as good as the list of names it is mailed to. It must be appropriate, up to date and personal – that is, addressed to a named individual, not "The Occupier" or "The Procurement Director". Database marketing is highly specialised and, though list-holding and its use are covered by data protection legislation in many countries, sources of relevant and high-quality lists are valuable. List building is often the reason for someone being asked to complete a survey or give their name and address. Lists can be bought or hired, thus avoiding the cost of creating and maintaining them. For instance, a magazine may sell its subscriber list to businesses wanting to promote to the same sort of people as the magazine's subscribers, which means in the case of competing products the first business to mail to those on the list may secure an advantage. Organisations that rent or sell their lists are often required by law or choose to ask their customers' permission to pass details to "carefully selected partners". For them to be truly useful, lists must be kept up to date and those paying to use them must seek assurances about accuracy; indeed, if individual addresses are out of date and material is returned, the contract with the list provider may include a clause whereby the fee for use of the list is reduced.

▶ The message. Skilful copywriting is crucial. Just one phrase changed may increase (or decrease) the response. When something is pulled out of an envelope, there are about three seconds during which the recipient decides whether or not to read on, so the message must have an immediate impact.

▶ The envelope. The "packaging" is part of the message. Many envelopes are overprinted, perhaps with a "teaser" message, and what is on them affects response. It is particularly important in getting the recipient to open the envelope and read the contents.

▶ The letter. A good message is as long as is necessary to present an argument to buy. If this takes two or three pages so be it; many letters are longer and still work well. As a general rule, a brochure of some sort plus a letter produces more responses than a brochure on its own.

▶ Brochures. These provide supporting information in many ways. They may be illustrated and often incorporate a range of incentives to respond such as prize draws.

Tiny details matter. For instance, a letter with a PS can generate more responses than one without; a reply card with a real postage stamp (rather than prepaid postage) may get up to 50% more replies; and certain so-called "magic" words (new, free, guaranteed, exciting) seem to boost response, provided they are not overused. Because direct mail is so testable, it is possible to try different things in different mailings (or split mailings so that parts of them are different in some way) and verify exactly what works best to promote a product.

Not all the copy – text, that is, whether in letter or brochure – may be read. People dip in and out of the material, so some repetition of content between, say, letters and brochures (though perhaps not word for word) is sensible. The relationship between what is said in different elements of the mail shot needs careful consideration.

Direct mail now overlaps with communication by e-mail. Spam (unsolicited mass e-mail) is now a tiresome fact of life, though junk mail filters have helped to isolate it, but e-mail to existing and lapsed customers (with their permission and giving people the ability to remove themselves from a list) can work well. Such communications, which are used by companies such as Amazon and Boden, always involve the ability to order online.

The major difference between a printed mail shot and e-mail is that reader attention spans are likely to be even shorter. It is easy to delete an e-mail in an instant, so the content must be punchy and pithy. It is also important to get the message across in the body of the e-mail; many people are suspicious of attachments (as they may carry viruses) and will not open them.

One point to bear in mind is that although repetition is fundamental to making a point stick, too much repetition becomes self-defeating. For instance, some mailing letters repeat the recipient's name several times within the text; once or twice may increase the personal feel, but too many times makes it seems like a contrived device and emphasises the sales nature of the communication.

To be successful both direct mail and e-mail require intelligent planning and research; they will not work without clarity of purpose and a sound base of information.

Sales promotion

Sales promotion is a part of marketing that provides an inducement aimed directly at persuading a target audience to achieve one or more of the company's defined objectives. In simpler terms, it is a method of persuading people to take a course of action that, without that persuasion, they would not otherwise take. Among what it encompasses are point-of-sale (POS) material such as window posters and shelf talkers, offers, giveaways, and merchandising and display in retail situations.

Sales promotion techniques are an aid to selling that should not be used simply because everyone else uses the same technique or because those who have run out of ideas think it is a good one. They are tactical techniques to be used because, after careful analysis of the facts and quantification of the objectives, it is thought they are likely to prove the most cost-effective methods of meeting objectives.

Yet perhaps because it is an "ideas" area, sales promotion activities are often based on an idea that in practice is flawed, which wastes resources and does not yield the desired results. But all businesses make mistakes in their marketing which hopefully they learn from.

The role of sales promotion in marketing

Sales promotion is part of the marketing mix and, like all other parts of the mix, has to be planned in the light of what it is meant to achieve, which might be to:

▶ introduce new products, by motivating customers to try a new product or intermediaries to accept it for resale (for example, introducing the idea of two products linked to sell together);

▶ attract new customers, by motivating potential customers to try a new product or retailers to stock it (for example, buying a particular product because of a competition they can enter);

▶ maintain competitiveness, by giving certain discounts or low prices preferentially to specific customers (or groups of customers). How this is presented affects the appeal – some may prefer a discount (the difference flagged, 10% off or whatever) and others a competitive price;

▶ increase sales in off-peak seasons, by encouraging consumption "out of season";

▶ increase the level of trade stocks, where appropriate, by special discounts or quantity purchasing allowances;

▶ induce present customers to buy more, by highlighting more ways and more occasions for using the product.

Generally, sales promotion aims to stimulate or re-stimulate demand for a product during a particular period. In the longer term, it cannot overcome deficiencies in a product's style, quality, packaging, design or function, but it can make a substantial difference to whether a product is successful or not.

A plethora of promotion

Almost by definition, a new promotional idea is thought up somewhere every minute of the day. Indeed, there are no hard and fast rules for selecting the "right" sales promotion tactic, since what is successful in one situation may not work in another.

In practice, there are likely to be many alternatives, all of which could be suitable for meeting the same objective. Selection can be assisted by studying what competitors do and answering such questions as:

▶ What are the disadvantages of each promotion tactic?

▶ Which promotion tactic best fits the profiles of the target audience(s)?

▶ What are the advantages and disadvantages of each promotion tactic?

▶ Which is likely to give the greatest level of success for the budget available?

▶ Which promotion best lends itself to accurate measurement of its effectiveness?

The many types of promotional tactic include those described below.

Promotions received at home or in the office

In-home consumer promotions can help to pre-empt competitors' attempts to solicit impulse purchases via in-store advertising and display. Techniques used include:

▶ sampling, where a sample of the product is delivered free to consumers' homes;

▶ coupon or voucher offers via postal and door-to-door distribution, newspaper or magazine distribution, and in-pack/ on-pack distribution;

▶ competitions.

In-store promotions

This type of promotion has the advantage that it is at the location where many final decisions and actual purchases are made. Techniques used include:

▶ temporary price reductions;

▶ extra value offers, including offers relating to future purchase (this includes store cards on which consumers collect points);

▶ premium offers (incentives), including free mail-in premiums (a coupon returned by customers that results in them being sent a free product sample or associated product or a gift. Thus a toothpaste manufacturer might send free toothpaste, mouthwash or a toothbrush), self-liquidating premiums (the consumer pays what appears to be – and may be – a good price but one that covers all the manufacturer's costs) and free gifts attached to products;

▶ point-of-sale product demonstrations;

▶ personality promotions (for example, with a demonstrator – as in toy shops – or a famous novelist signing his latest book).

Immediate benefit promotions

Here, consumer reward for purchasing is immediate. Usually the sooner the reward can be expected and received after the qualifying action, the more sales will be prompted. Techniques used include:

▶ temporary price reductions;

▶ free gifts (which can be additional product, such as two for the price of one);

▶ banded pack offers (for instance a new razor with shaving soap);

▶ economy (special editions and own-brand items).

Some of these are offered as part of other broader schemes. For example, airline "mileage" points can sometimes be redeemed for products other than those supplied by the airline, such as hotel accommodation or car hire; Marriott Hotels boasts that its rewards scheme offers 250 ways to use points.

Trade promotions

Some promotions are directed exclusively at intermediary organisations or their staff. Reasons for promoting to the trade include:

▶ obtaining support and co-operation in stocking and promoting products to customers;

▶ inducing distributors to increase their stock levels, where research may have revealed lower-than-average stockholding;

▶ pre-empting competitive selling activities by increasing trade stocks.

Among the techniques used in trade promotion are:

▶ bonusing – can take the form of monetary discounts or "free goods" (13 products for the price of 12), or special quantity terms;

▶ incentive schemes – can be tailored to the needs of a retailer's sales staff and may also include competitions, particularly for sales staff – for example, competitions linked to generating window displays with prizes such as holidays;

▶ dealer loaders – instead of money, gift incentives may be offered to distributors, or their sales force, for achieving agreed sales targets or stocking certain quantities of a product.

Other trade promotions which are aimed at increasing the visibility of the product include:

▶ Co-operative advertising schemes. These help in preparing advertisements or sharing media costs, which in some businesses make possible promotional activity that might not happen unsupported. This occurs, for instance, in the travel industry with an airline and a hotel promoting a package involving both their products.

▶ Providing (possibly on a shared-cost basis) display materials, such as display stands, posters and shelf talkers (small signs that go on the shelf where the product is displayed).

▶ Tailor-made promotions. These are custom designed to an outlet's individual requirements, often promoting its own name and corporate image.

For many products, trade promotions are important in helping to make sure that the product is in the shops or otherwise available for sale at the right time – and is actively promoted at the point of sale.

Sales promotion in action

Sales promotion was pioneered in the fast-moving consumer goods (FMCG) market but it is used much more widely – albeit in slightly different ways. Thus sales promotion might be needed to:

▶ encourage repeat purchase;

▶ secure occasional buyers;

▶ combat competitive action;

▶ make sure that bills are paid on time (for instance, offering better terms if bills are paid on time or discounts linked to early payment);

▶ motivate retailers and their sales people;

▶ induce rapid market penetration when launching a new product or service;

▶ sustain perception of value over and above that intrinsically possessed by the product itself;

▶ smooth out costly buying cycles and seasonality (promotion is designed to prompt sales at a time of otherwise low purchase, for instance deals to encourage people to buy, say, garden furniture ahead of the summer season).

Promotions do not always yield the desired results but they out-perform expectations; most are variations on a well-tried rather than a unique idea. In consumer goods marketing often 70% of budgets are spent on sales promotion with the remaining 30% spent on advertising.

Display and merchandising

This is the term used for the promotional effect of layout and display in retailers of all sorts, though elements of it may be just as important in an industrial showroom. A strong window display can make people want to look inside the shop. In a supermarket, essentials such as bread are often at the back of the store, so customers have to pass many other, less essential, items on the way to those they need to buy.

The phrase "impulse buy" is used to describe unplanned purchases made on the spur of the moment because something catches someone's eye. This is not a way of making people buy something they do not want, so much as a way of making sure they buy sooner rather than later and from somewhere else. So things that need some promoting generally go at the front of the shop.

Merchandising and display have clear objectives, and research confirms they have a powerful influence on purchasing decisions. They are designed to:

▶ Sell more – selling a quantity over and above the level that would occur if no action were taken. Some people will always want certain products and will search them out.

▶ Inform the customer about various matters in various ways – telling them a shop is there, indicating something of the range of products it sells, highlighting what is new, directing people to the right section of the shop, and so on.

▶ Persuade – making the message attractive, understandable and convincing, special. This aspect can prompt the action that is really wanted – a sale.

Merchandising and display influence three groups in particular:

▶ those who may pass the shop by and will not even enter unless something external catches their eye;

▶ those who come into the shop for one small item and who may buy more, and the ubiquitous "browser"; so shops that attract browsers stock a range of different things (as in the case of bookshops);

▶ those who are regular customers.

There are all sorts of people in each category: young, old, richer, poorer, male, female and so on. Because of their different intentions, some merchandising and display messages will be general; others will be specific, aimed exclusively at one group or another. In addition, there are the products themselves. The promotional and display permutations are numerous, and in shops such as DIY stores there may be thousands of lines stocked.

Any change of products to be sold (and therefore displayed), coupled with the customers' tendency to notice only what is new, means displays must regularly be changed or updated if they are to freshen people's interest.

Achieving impact

Display must therefore be carefully carried out to achieve the right effect. Marketers have a mnemonic, AIDA, which demonstrates what must be done:

▶ A – catch the customers' attention

▶ I – arouse their interest

▶ D – turn their interest into desire

▶ A - prompt action

This is the essential principle behind all good display, and checking a particular display to see if it will carry customers through this kind of sequence is a useful test of its likely effectiveness. All sorts of interesting combinations are usually possible, and ringing the changes and regularly surprising people works well.

The contribution of shop layout

Physical store layout is a science in itself. Some aspects are fixed for a variety of reasons, such as cost or the lease will not allow change and so on. Others are not and certain basic principles of layout are an important part of the promotional mix. Examples of display considerations are as follows:

▶ Traffic flow. 90% of the population are right-handed and will turn left on entering a shop and go round it clockwise. Most retailers organise for this.

▶ Eyes. Customers select most readily from goods displayed at eye level (60–62 inches/1.52–1.57m for a woman, a little higher for a man). This puts high or low shelves at a corresponding disadvantage; and many shops have plenty of both. There are problems here with the volume of stock to be carried and displayed, but customers resent bending down to shop and if things are out of reach, people are reluctant to "be a nuisance" by asking for them and may not buy.

▶ Quantity. Customers buy more readily from things displayed in quantity rather than a single example of a product.

▶ Vertical display. Products displayed together are more manageable if they are above and below each other rather than arranged side by side.

▶ Accident. Customers are less likely to pick up from, or browse, a layout that appears accident-prone – that is, if they think that inspecting something may risk other items falling and being damaged. This is important in shops where customers need to pick up and inspect products.

▶ Choice. Customers are attuned to choice. Displaying a number of options makes this easy to exercise – products sell better from within a range of similar items.

▶ Relationships. Customers expect to find related items close at hand (so batteries close to battery-powered toys – clever combinations may help).

▶ Checkouts. These need to be convenient and clearly indicated (and, of course, promptly and helpfully manned) and can be a focal point for some display.

▶ Position. In a large shop, people will walk or search further for things they feel are essential. So if children's clothes are up a flight of stairs and there is no elevator, mothers with pushchairs may not make that shop their first choice.

▶ Colour. This has a fashion, and an image, connotation – bright may be seen as brash – so careful selection is required. This applies to display materials, such as a backcloth in the window, as well as decoration. Too dull, however, and it is not noticed.

▶ Lighting. This must be good because if something cannot be seen clearly no one will buy it – people's patience is limited.

▶ Seating. Some shops want to encourage browsing, so if lack of space does not prohibit it, they provide some chairs, as many bookshops do, or seating for those accompanying shoppers who may otherwise curtail the time they spend in the store.

▶ Background music. This evokes strong opinions. Some like it; some hate it. However, a library-like silence can be off-putting for some. The volume needs careful consideration. Starbucks displays a notice to tell customers what is playing and aims to sell copies of the CD.

▶ Character. Part of the overall atmosphere will come from the décor and fixtures and fittings; the mood created by them needs to reflect the image that the store wants to project.

▶ Floor. This will be noticed. Is it quiet? Can it be kept clean easily? Does it (or should it) direct customer flow as some shops do, using different colours for pathways?

▶ Signs. People are reluctant to ask so there must be sufficient signs, and all must be clear and direct people easily to everything in the shop. In addition, many signs are virtually in-store advertisements and can be used to good effect, especially if they are striking or unusual. Too many signs, however, can be confusing, especially if they mask each other.

▶ Standing space. Space to stand back and look without blocking "traffic" flow will encourage purchase; people will not go where they are likely to be bumped into.

▶ Inconvenience. Some stores feel that their offering is sufficiently strong to organise things so that although customers may suffer some inconvenience, they enhance the sales opportunities. For example, in IKEA stores customers must walk past everything to reach the exit.

All of this must fit in with the security arrangements necessary to prevent crime. The overall physical construction and layout are the backcloth to any display, in a shop or in the window. Merchandising demonstrates the need to leave no promotional corner ineffective.

Lastly, this is an area that can demonstrate the bizarre nature of customer behaviour. For instance, smell can trigger sales – a supermarket will sell more fresh bread if the aroma of baking pervades the store. The reason may be known only to scientists, but if this sort of thing works, and it does, marketers will use it.

Electronic promotion

The internet, e-mail, mobile phones and the electronic revolution in general have transformed our daily lives and brought a new and ever-changing dimension to marketing. To some extent it is only the way of doing things that is changing. A website, for instance, fulfils the same role as a brochure or catalogue, but in many cases it also acts as a distribution channel as in the case of e-retailers such as Amazon – and it allows for much more interaction between the retailer and the customer. But the e-transformation has brought with it new costs and threats. All businesses now have to have websites, which cost money to set up and take time and money to maintain. The other side of the coin is that the economics of e-retailing and increased price transparency have put downward pressure on prices for products and services.

In banking, the ATM and internet banking have transformed the way people access and handle their accounts. In retailing, after registering the sale, the electronic till communicates with stock control, allowing more supplies to be ordered automatically when they fall below a set level.

When a customer uses certain cards (especially those now referred to as "smart" cards) the sale can be recorded against an individual, as is the case with loyalty cards. Customers may then start to receive promotions through the post for those or other products (stores charge their suppliers to send out mail shots on their behalf). This allows offer coupons to be distributed to particular customers in a way that reflects their buying record, or rather influences their future buying.

But such changes can cause problems for marketers. For example, because it can monitor sales of every product and reorder electronically, a retailer may be less willing to see sales people, who then have to find new ways of prompting the discussions they want. Such discussions go a long way beyond reordering and involve promotion, display and much else, and are crucial to the marketing effort. As more and more buying decisions are made centrally, meetings with the central buyers can be the only way of influencing sales to many outlets.

Despite greater complexity, there have been huge advantages. Examples of what has become normal include the following:

▶ Computers can now calculate optimum merchandising arrangements. A company making a range of products that differ in size, price, margin and rates of turnover can work out quickly what mix of products should be put on any particular length of shelving allocated to its brand. No space is left on the shelf and turnover and profit generation are maximised.

▶ Field sales staff routinely carry computers and use them to give instant answers to customer questions about stock and delivery of a product.

▶ Customer details can be accessed instantly during transactions. This helps with many processes, for example dealing at a distance from a call centre.

Technological developments will produce many more advances of this sort, all either actively assisting marketing effort, or to which marketing must adapt if it is to remain successful.

Electronic marketing

The internet and e-commerce are well established and have a significant but sometimes overstated influence on promotion and distribution.

Promotion

For all their technical wizardry, websites are only another method of communicating with customers (and sometimes of doing business). The website may be an electronic addition (or even alternative) to a brochure, a sales person, a showroom or shop. First and foremost, a website is a promotional channel. As such, it must command attention, put over its message clearly and persuade. It must also be convenient and easy to use (to navigate) for people with differing levels of computer literacy.

The internet has become an increasingly important advertising medium. Examples of the form it takes include the following:

▶ A simple brochure-style website may have integral advertisements and pop-ups (small ads that appear over part of a revealed page).

▶ A shop-style website, such as Amazon's, has many advertisements for its own allied product sales and for other suppliers as different as, say, insurance and cars.

▶ A portal, such as Microsoft's MSN, has many advertisements and links to other suppliers, large, such as eBay, and small. Between them, Hotmail (Microsoft's e-mail operation) and Yahoo! have nearly 500m users. No wonder there are many marketers who want to advertise on them, especially those who also canvass business direct in a way that enables customers to click on their advertisement, move to their site and place an order.

Distribution

Doing business, or e-commerce, via the internet has grown hugely in the past decade. In this case the point about clarity and convenience is perhaps even more important. Again, it is an area of rapid change, and one that has had a substantial impact on conventional retailing.

Some transactions work well exclusively through the internet. For example, someone who wants the latest novel by a favourite author may simply visit Amazon, call up the title and place the order (perhaps comparing prices along the way). The same is true of car or travel insurance, but these are often bought through internet comparison sites. Other purchases are more complex. For instance, someone who wants a new CD player, say, may well first do some research on the internet about models but then want to assess sound quality, and so visits a retail store, where he may be persuaded to buy because of immediate availability – or he may later search the internet, visiting a price comparison site to see if it can be bought more cheaply online.

More and more people are doing their supermarket shopping online. Bulk goods, from detergent to cat food, and regular items can be ordered over the internet and delivered. Some customers only visit stores for things that demand real choice or checking.

Customer focus

To be successful, websites must be customer focused. This may seem obvious. But it also means that they should not necessarily incorporate everything that is technologically possible (perhaps just because someone regards that as a challenge), or be comprehensive or interactive in every way – though, of course, different sites aim at people with differing levels of technical competence.

All websites should be designed with the people who will use them firmly in mind, to work in the way they want, or at least find they like, and to do so efficiently. People will quickly give up on a site they find difficult to navigate. Website content and design send a strong message about an organisation. People will notice how a site works (not least compared with others), they will talk about it to other people and they will elect to log on again – or not. Image is affected; so are future business prospects. So setting up the website needs care and consideration – and then it needs regular review.

Developing web operations

When developing a website it is important to be clear about what it is there to do, the money to be spent on it and the time it will take to set up, maintain and keep up to date.

In the early days of websites there were many organisations that spent large amounts of time and money to no good effect. But websites have become slicker and more focused and the profusion of them provides plenty of models from which to learn.

Objectives

When considering the specific objectives of any website development, two particular purposes predominate:

▶ A reference point. A website may be partly a source of reference, for people to consult to obtain information (and be impressed by it at the same time). For example, many accountants have sites providing current tax information or rates. Or it may play a more integral part in the overall sales and marketing process. In this case, its effectiveness must be measured by counting the number of new contacts it produces and, in turn, how many of those are, in due course, turned into paying customers.

▶ An ordering point. A website may exist so that people can order and pay for products directly through it. For example, a consultancy might offer for sale a survey of some sort, primarily as an example of its expertise and style (though it might also be a source of revenue). A product company might, of course, have its whole range listed and available to order from the site. In this case, not only must the ordering system work well (it must be quick and easy for the customer), but the follow-up must also be good. An initial good impression will quickly evaporate if the order takes too long to arrive or needs chasing. It is a mistake to demand too much information from the buyer as an order is placed. People like the online ordering process to be simple and to give them a chance to change their mind, and, if they are repeat purchasers, they do not want to give all their personal details again. There also needs to be an efficient and easy to use returns process should the customer not be happy with the product.

Three tasks

Once clear objectives are set, three distinct tasks must be fulfilled:

▶ Attract people to the site. Although most people assume all organisations have a website, its existence does not mean that they will log on to it in droves or that they will be the type of people wanted. Most businesses now include website details on corporate stationery and promotional material.

▶ Impress people when they see it. This includes its presentation, content and ease of use. It means keeping a close eye on customers' views and accommodating all the necessary practicalities as it is set up. For example, all sorts of impressive images and graphics are possible. They can look good and provide useful information. But if they take a long time to download, visitors to the site may find it tedious and log off.

▶ Encourage repeat use. This, too, is a likely objective. If it is, efforts must be made to encourage further contact (again using a range of prompts), which may overlap with other forms of communication. (For example, getting purchasers to sign up for news e-mails and so on.)

There are also other considerations:

▶ Site content – what should be presented (this is a continuous job, not a one-off).

▶ Interaction – how contacting the website can prompt the kind of dialogue desired (if any).

▶ Topicality – how up to date it should be (this affects how regularly it needs revising).

▶ Ease of use – its convenience and accessibility (does it have a suitable navigation mechanism?).

▶ Image – how can it affect the brand image and will it look consistent (and not as if it has been put together by different people in different ways)?

▶ Security – the protection it needs (for example, is customer confidentiality protected, is it vulnerable to hackers?).

Overall, creating a website needs at least the same level of planning, co-ordination and careful execution as any other form of marketing communication; because of the pace of change in website technology and design it may need even more. It is also likely to need active co-operation from people within the organisation who will provide and update information. This may be a larger job than it first appears, not just because of the numbers involved, but also because they may have differing perspectives (with, say, research and marketing differing about the depth of technical information that should be included). Responsibility for the site and what it contains must be unequivocally allocated, together with the appropriate authority to see things through. Practical solutions are needed to meet clear objectives and these should always be customer focused.

Further considerations

Technological advance will continue to bring new opportunities and support to website marketing. Recent developments include the following:

▶ Linking in research. Software packages allow regular research and formal monthly analysis about who is using a website, their characteristics, and how and why they contact the site. It allows the way the system works to be tailored to the needs of an individual user. The intention is to obtain information that will make the website a more accurate and effective marketing tool.

▶ Linking to sales. Similarly, there are systems that allow a visitor to a website to click in a way that prompts a response from the organisation to discuss some specific detail of an offer. This can be instant and online, so that both parties can look at the site on screen and discuss it. Alternatively, a telephone call is made. This is essentially a sales call. If the process is made sufficiently easy, it will generate conversations that can influence the likelihood of sales which might otherwise never occur.

▶ Utilising appropriate technology. Some applications are particularly well-suited to a specific product or service. For example, it is possible to book a hotel following a detailed inspection of it over the internet. Before long it will be possible to do this in a way that is almost as real as walking around the actual building. This is what many people want. If an alternative to actually visiting a hotel is provided, something that is judged by potential customers as better than any sort of brochure, a particular provider will have an edge against its competitors.

Electronic marketing is an area that is constantly changing. Viral marketing (see page 148) exploits the way in which people use the internet. If message or video clip uploaded to a website such as YouTube is found to be fun, informative or amusing, word of mouth (WOM) will rapidly increase viewings of it. As an indication of the power of WOM, in 2009 more than 20m people worldwide viewed a clip of Susan Boyle singing on a UK television show, *Britain's Got Talent*. YouTube immediately proposed changes to the site that would allow more advertising to be featured.

Digital word of mouth

Digital WOM is useful and powerful. Nielsen, a market research firm, showed that in 2007, 78% of customers trusted consumer recommendations more than anything else they were exposed to in marketing. In 2008, to stop this being abused, astroturfing (placing messages that appear to have a source other than their real one) was prohibited under European law. Sony, for example, suffered bad publicity when it was revealed that a fan site had been set up by the company; people do not like it if something that appears to be non-commercial is in fact commercial. Yet organisations are spending an increasing amount of time and money in this area. Borders, a book retailer, which has run campaigns using social networking site Facebook, accepts the dynamic nature of this area and regards WOM as "a bit of a minefield", according to Nick Atkinson, Borders' Digital Marketing Manager; but it is working at it and getting good results. Other large companies, including Burger King and JCPenny, have also used Facebook. Just as with other forms of marketing, accurate targeting is the key, and numerous specialist agencies are springing up to create and guide initiatives and to measure results.

Social networking

If messages are honest and transparent, if they create what in the jargon is called "engagement" (that is, they involve people whose actions then extend what is being done) and if they are well tailored to the networks they address (or rather the people who make up those networks), they can add constructively to more conventional forms of marketing in a way that is truly additive. The technical devices that assist this process are many and varied. A current favourite is widgets – small bundles of software that can add movement, especially in the form of graphics, to enhance the message. They may well enhance, but they do not necessarily transform. Logging onto Facebook could be compared to walking into a bar where there are lots of friends and acquaintances; a widget could be thought of as the bar having pleasant background music. It can enhance the experience, but it is not the prime influence on your judgment of the whole experience. The task for marketers is to watch such developments, use what is helpful and constantly watch for more; the fast-moving nature of this area should never be underestimated.

The social networking scene is changing remarkably fast. Facebook, which started in 2004, had over 200m users worldwide some four years later having overtaken MySpace, which was set up in 2003. Among later social networks has been Twitter, which in 2009 had the fastest growth rate of all social networking sites, proving that users are always looking for something new.

Selecting the promotional mix

The variety of promotional methods means that selecting the right mix and implementing the promotional activity are complex. So too is deciding how much to spend. Huge amounts of money were wasted on internet development and marketing during the dotcom boom years. Clearly success, in terms of promotion of any sort that works, does not just happen; a systematic approach is necessary, as is a degree of formality (a 12-step approach was discussed in Chapter 8). The organisation must also consider what financial resources can be allocated to promotion.

Setting the promotional budget

This must run in parallel with deciding what to do. There are several approaches to the complex issue of setting a promotional budget, as described below.

Percentage of sales

This takes a fixed percentage, usually based on forecast sales, and relies on the questionable assumption that there is always a direct relationship between promotional expenditure and sales; the budget is simply calculated as a percentage of the sales revenue. Similarly, if a 15% increase in sales is forecast, this assumes that a 15% increase in promotional effort is required. This rationale may not be real as it will depend on many factors other than expenditure. Thus it is probably the least effective, but the traditional and easiest approach.

Competitive parity approach

This involves spending a similar amount on promotion as competitors, or maintaining the same proportion of expenditure as the industry average for similar organisations. This assumes that market share will be retained. However, competitors may take a different promotional approach and thus the costs are not comparable. A view about what is being done in a competitive industry may well be useful, but the danger is that this becomes the "collective wisdom" and the blind may end up leading the blind. Competitors' expenditure cannot ever be more than an indication of their budgets. For strategic reasons it may be that a budget should be either greater than that of a competitor or set lower. No two organisations pursue identical objectives from the same base line of resources and market standing, and it is wrong to assume that all competitors will spend equally or to the same effect.

Combination of percentage of sales and competitive parity

This is a more comprehensive approach but does not overcome the inherent problems of each method. It does recognise the need for profitability and takes into account the impact of competitor expenditure.

What is affordable?

If the optimum spend cannot be objectively decided, whatever money is available must suffice. Therefore marketers must know:

▶ what sums are available after all costs have been accounted for;

▶ the cash position of the business as a whole;

▶ the revenue forecast.

In some organisations advertising and promotion are left to share out the tail end of the budget, with greater expenditure being equated with lower profits (especially where accountants have supremacy). Others take the view that at least in some instances more expenditure on promotion might lead to more sales at marginal cost, which, in turn, would lead to higher profits overall.

Fixed sum per sales unit

This method is similar to percentage of sales, except that a specific amount per unit is used, rather than a percentage of sales value. In this way money for promotional purposes is not affected by changes in price, reflecting a view that promotional expenditure is an investment, not merely a cost.

What has been learnt from previous years?

When setting next year's budget businesses start by looking at this year's budget against actual performance. Were the results as forecast? What is happening in the market and will it continue? What effect is this having, and what repercussions will this have?

Marketers wisely:

▶ experiment, testing and measuring different parts of a market to see whether expenditure appears to be to low to achieve what is wanted or money is being wasted;

▶ monitor results, by tracking the awareness of promotions among customers; this can be relatively easy, and the results of experiments with different budget levels can then be used in planning the next step (always bearing in mind that all other things do not remain the same).

Task method approach

In the light of the weaknesses of other approaches, a more comprehensive four-step procedure is possible, whereby the emphasis is on the tasks involved in implementing a promotional strategy. The four steps are to:

▶ analyse the market – from the facts a promotional approach can be decided and a strategy developed;

▶ determine objectives – from the analysis, set clear short- and long-term promotional objectives for the continuity and build-up of promotional impact and effect;

▶ identify promotional tasks – determine the promotional activities required to achieve the marketing and promotional objectives;

▶ cost identified promotional tasks – calculate the likely cost of each element in the communications mix and the cost-effectiveness of each element.

Choosing the media

What media are likely to be chosen and what is the target (the number of advertisements, leaflets and so on) that must be considered?

In advertising, for example, the media schedule can easily be converted into an advertising budget by adding space or time costs to the costs of devising the advertising material. The overall promotional budget is usually determined by costing the expenses of preparing and distributing promotional material and so on. A variety of options may need to be considered, balancing greater or lesser expenditure against larger or smaller returns. In other words, the tasks must be specified and costed. With this done, a budget will be firmly grounded. The great advantage of this budgetary approach compared with others is that it is comprehensive, systematic and likely to be more realistic. However, other methods can still be used to provide "ball-park" estimates, although they may produce disparate answers. For example:

▶ we can afford $12,000;

▶ the task requires $15,500;

▶ to match the competition requires $18,500;

▶ last year's spending was $9,500.

The decision now becomes a matter of value judgment, making allowance for overall company philosophy and objectives. There is no accurate, mathematical or automatic method of determining the promotional budget. The task method, however, is probably the most accurate, if not the easiest.

In a large organisation, or one with a substantial promotional budget, this will be done in conjunction with an advertising agency, which will carry out tasks such as media buying or providing the creative input. Such budget setting is an integral part of planning the mix of promotional activity.

Key points

▶ Promotion encompasses a number of techniques which need to be deployed in the right mix; against sound, well-co-ordinated objectives; and creatively.

▶ Originality and creativity are crucial to successful promotion. An inexpensive, creative and original approach can (and often does) score over a high-budget, stereotyped, unimaginative approach.

▶ Advertising can never sell a poor product (certainly not more than once), but a well thought-out and consistent approach can become memorable, prompt sales and hold off competitors.

▶ Advertising is a fragile process and even the best planned campaigns can be destroyed by circumstances. For example, in 2003 the Hong Kong Tourist Board was about to launch a campaign based on the slogan "Hong Kong: it takes your breath away!" just as the SARS epidemic started. The campaign was stopped in time but the money spent on it was wasted.

▶ Even if half the money spent on promotion is wasted, what the other half achieves is important.

12

Personal persuasive influences

*Our goal as a company is to have customer
service that is not just the best, but legendary.*

Sam Walton, founder, Wal-Mart

Promotion – in all its forms and however good – can be wasted if
it is not backed by effective sales and service. In many industries
(especially in industrial and business-to-business marketing), promotional activity rarely produces actual business. That is not to say
that it is useless; rather its job is to create interest. Turning that interest into orders is the job of sales, and the work of sales people is
the only part of the marketing process that involves direct personal
persuasive contact. Such meetings can take place in many locations: in a customer's home or workplace or on neutral territory.
Selling is important in completing the marketing process; so too is
another area of personal customer communication – the style and
effectiveness of customer service.

The nature of personal persuasion

Selling sometimes suffers from an unfortunate image. Instant judgments on, say, a double-glazing or insurance sales person often
include the words "pushy" or "high pressure". Selling can be associated with pushing inappropriate goods on reluctant customers.

The most effective selling is through "helping people to buy".
Much of it has advisory overtones and, if it is to be acceptable as
well as effective, it cannot be pushy, but must, like everything in

marketing, be customer oriented. Selling is a skilled job. Customers may want the product, but with plenty of alternative sources of supply they are demanding; convincing them to do business with a particular supplier may be no easy task. IBM is said to train every sales person to deal with customers as if they were on the verge of walking away.

At one end of the scale selling is simple, just a question. For example, a store selling liquor may be able to increase sales significantly by making sure that every time staff behind the counter are asked for liquor they say: "How many mixers do you want?" Many people will respond positively to what has been called the "gin and tonic" effect, the linking of one product with another. Sometimes the question is even simpler. For example, the waiter in a hotel or bar who says "Another drink?" is selling, and the server in McDonald's who says "Large fries?" is selling up, attempting to get customers to pay more than they originally intended. Such action should be easy to implement – just an instruction to staff.

But sales often do not come from the success of one interaction with the customer. A chain of events is involved, several people, a period of time and, importantly, a cumulative effect. In other words, each stage, perhaps involving some combination of meetings, proposals, presentations and more meetings, must go well or the customer will not move on to the next.

What is necessary will vary depending on circumstances, but the stages and some of the principles involved throughout the sales process do have some commonality.

Selling starts, logically enough, with identifying the people to whom to sell. Sales time is expensive, so it is important for sales people to spend time with genuine prospects, even more so when the lead time is long, which is typical in the purchase of, say, computer systems. In some industries sales people spend most of their time dealing with regular customers. In others, the place of contact may be regular but the people may change frequently, so new relationships must be built. A constant supply of new potential customers is important. Some of the right people come forward as a result of promotional activity. They phone or respond to a mail shot or website, and in so doing they are saying "tell me more". More have to be found and finding them is the first stage of the selling process.

Locating prospects

A prospecting process must, where necessary, produce a constant stream of new names. A variety of sources can be tapped, ranging from directories and trade bodies to exhibitions and the press. One or a combination of these can supply valuable information about prospects: the names of companies; what business they are in; if it is going well or badly; whether they export; how big they are; who owns them; what subsidiaries or associates they have; and last, but certainly not least, who runs and manages them.

Who is then approached is crucial, and this may not be a simple decision. Indeed, it may be that more than one person is involved. For example, for business clients of a travel agent, the following must be considered: the person in charge of travel purchasing in an organisation (perhaps a person in the procurement department of a large company); the person who travels; the person who sends them; and perhaps also the person who makes the booking. Many personal assistants have considerable discretionary power in making travel bookings, and not least among their considerations will be how straightforward and easy they find a travel agency to deal with.

As well as considering which individual to approach, the other important assessment at this stage is financial potential. How much business might be obtained from a prospect in, say, a year? This analysis will rule out some prospects as not being worth further pursuit. Experience will increase the accuracy with which these decisions can be made, but meanwhile a good first list is developing. The military maxim that "time spent in reconnaissance is seldom wasted" is a good one. In war it can help to prevent casualties; in business it not only produces information, in this case on who should be contacted, but it also provides a platform for a more accurately conceived, and more successful, approach.

Having identified whom to contact, the next step is to organise the approach.

The method of approach

The ultimate objective is almost certainly a face-to-face meeting, which must be held before any substantial business can result. Such a meeting may occur as a result of:

▶ cold calling, that is, calling without an appointment (a technique that has limited application these days and needs care);

▶ sending a letter, card or e-mail (not spam) with or without supporting literature;

▶ telephoning "cold" or as a follow-up to a letter or promotion;

▶ getting people together, initially as a group, and making a presentation at the organisation's premises, a hotel or other venue, or through a third party (such as at a trade body meeting).

The logistics are also important. What is needed is a campaign spread over time so that when favourable responses occur, they can be followed up promptly, which may not be possible if there are many within a short period.

Who will take the action

The approach needs to be made by people who will be perceived as being appropriate – that is, have the right status in terms of the person being approached. They will also need the right attitude, wanting to win business in what may be a new and perhaps difficult area. And they need the knowledge and skills to tackle the task in hand: knowledge of the customers, of their own organisation and its products and so on backed by more technical elements where appropriate.

The initial approach

In making the approach, detail is important, as are skills in customer contact, writing sales letters, selling, negotiation and so on. The initial approach is crucial, as is any first impression, and so needs to be thought through carefully. There may be no second chance. In any meeting or conversation, the sales person must quickly understand the potential buyer's personality and stance in order to make their pitch both persuasive and acceptable – not so "pushy" as to be self-defeating.

The sales process

Selling goes through various stages. It starts with an understanding of the buyer. No one can sell effectively without understanding how people make decisions to purchase. A good way of thinking about it, one originated by psychologists in the United States, suggests that the decision-making goes through seven distinct stages which can be paraphrased as:

▶ I am important and I want to be respected.

▶ Consider my needs.

▶ How will your ideas help me?

▶ What are the facts?

▶ What are the snags?

▶ What shall I do?

▶ I approve.

Customers must do what they feel is necessary to make a decision; indeed, the way selling is conducted must allow this to happen. Success factors in closing the sale (obtaining a commitment to buy) are matching the buyer's progress through the decision-making process described above, describing the product in a well-considered way and discussing it in relation to what a particular buyer needs.

The basics of successful selling

To be successful, sales staff must:

▶ Plan. They must see the right people, the right number of people, regularly if necessary.

▶ Prepare. Sales contact needs to be thought through (the so called "born sales person" is rare; the best of the rest do their homework and benefit from it).

▶ Understand the customer. They must deploy empathy (the ability to put themselves in the customer's shoes), base what they do on real needs and be seen to do so.

▶ Project in the appropriate manner. Not every sales person is welcome, and not everyone can position themselves as an adviser or whatever makes their approach acceptable. Being accepted needs to be worked at.

▶ Conduct a good meeting. They must stay in control, direct the contact, yet make the customer like it. What is said must be understandable, attractive and credible if it is to persuade.

▶ Listen. A much undervalued skill in selling.

▶ Handle objections. The pros and cons need debating; selling is not about winning arguments or scoring points.

▶ Be persistent. They must ask for a commitment, and, if necessary ask again.

In most specialist companies there will be special skills that sales staff must deploy. In pharmaceuticals, for example, many factors are important. With an extensive product range (which may number thousands), acquiring the necessary product knowledge is more difficult than for those in a company selling a single product, especially if it is not technical. Time is probably the most important factor – doctors allow medical representatives little time to make their case and they may have only one or two minutes to describe a single medicine. A sales person who cannot make a succinct and powerful case for the product cannot do the job.

Additional skills

Other skills that may be necessary include:

▶ account analysis and planning;

▶ the writing skills necessary for proposal/quotation documents to be as persuasive as face-to-face contact;

▶ formal presentation;

▶ numeracy and negotiation.

All this is required in a job in which people are sometimes

described as being "only in sales". Furthermore, whether a customer buys again, and buys more, will depend primarily on two other things:

▶ Service. It almost goes without saying, but promises of service made by sales people must be fulfilled. If they are not, the customer will notice. Many people may be involved in servicing an account. They all have to appreciate the importance of getting their bit right. If customers are promised information by 3.30pm, a brochure in today's post, two suggested proposals in writing and a call to follow up, they should get just that. Even minor variations, such as information by 4pm, matter. Promising what can be done, and doing it to the letter, is very much part of selling; exceeding expectations differentiates powerfully.

▶ Follow-up. Even if they receive first-class service, customers must continue to be sold to after ordering and contact must be maintained in a variety of ways (without it becoming irritating).

A follow-up programme of this sort can improve the chances of repeat business and make sure that opportunities to sell more products or services are not missed.

Sales management

It is not enough for a company simply to push sales people out into the field and say "sell". Sales people must be managed just like anyone else. Usually a sales manager is part of the overall marketing team or, in a small company, the role may be undertaken by an owner or general manager.

The person managing the sales team will usually handle a certain number of customers, usually the large ones, personally because they demand the attention of the company's most senior representative, who in any case should have the best chance of selling to them. This also helps sales managers get a better idea of reaction to the product(s), which is important in managing the team.

The classic tasks of sales management generally fall into six areas:

▶ Plan. Spend time planning the scope and extent of the sales operation, its budget and what it aims to achieve. Achievement is organised first around targets. Setting targets, not just for the amount to be sold, but also for profitability, product mix and so on, is an important task. If the product range is large, it is especially important that the team's activities are directed with the right focus.

▶ Organise. Calculate the number of sales people required (allowing for cost, customer service and coverage), as well as how and where they are deployed. This must also address the question of the various market sectors involved, looking at not just who calls on customers in, say, Hertfordshire or Manhattan, but how major accounts are dealt with and the strategy for any non-traditional outlets that may need separate consideration. Organisations selling to groups of customers that differ radically from each other may separate the different sales tasks and even have separate sales teams, as do large companies (such as Unilever) for their many brands.

▶ Staff. It is no good, as they say, "paying peanuts and employing monkeys". To deliver the best results, put time and effort into recruiting and selecting the best possible team.

▶ Develop. Because there is no single "right" way to sell, deploy the appropriate approach day by day, meeting by meeting, customer by customer, and continually fine tune both the approaches and the skills that generate them over the long term. If the team is to be professional in this sense, it will require more than a brief induction; a process of field development is necessary.

▶ Motivate. Constantly make sure that people not only can do what is required, but will also want to excel.

▶ Control. As with any other kind of management, it is important to control and fine tune action.

Overall, the quality of sales management is often readily discernible from the performance of the sales team.

Sales productivity

Whatever quality is brought to the conduct of sales calls, productivity matters, too. The crucial variables are:

▶ who is seen (the selection of appropriate prospects, buyers or customers);

▶ how many people are seen;

▶ how often they are seen (the call frequency decided upon and how it varies and is used).

If these productivity factors are well organised, and worked at on a regular basis, overall results are likely to be improved. Sales productivity comes first from seeing the right people. This may mean sales people having to see several people in an organisation's different departments (as in selling, say, training services to a company where purchases might be made by the human resources, training or functional departments). Or it might just mean finding out who is the real decision-maker.

Sales productivity also comes from sheer quantity; the more people are seen the more orders are obtained. If a sales person makes an average of five calls per day instead of four, that is around 200 extra calls per year, and if quality is maintained, it would be surprising if this did not result in more orders.

Then there is the question of frequency of contact. The rule is to call the minimum number of times that will preserve and build the business. Some accounts are contacted every week; others may be seen only once a year. Whatever the circumstance, judging the right call frequency needs thought.

Monitoring the numbers involved all along the line can influence action and results. For instance, a target for the number of prospecting calls to be made, the number of sales calls to be scheduled and conducted, the frequency of calling on regular customers and so on are prescriptive: they prompt action that will make it more likely that targets for the amount and value of products to be sold are achieved.

Account management

All customers are different. The way most marketers categorise them is by size – the amount of actual or potential business they produce. Major accounts then need special treatment. In many markets there are only a few major players, just one of which might be worth, say, 25% of the business of a company selling fast-moving consumer goods. Thus:

▶ Companies have people with titles such as "major account manager" who are responsible for winning business with just a few major customers.

▶ Major customer strategies need to be set. In other words, a plan for creating, maintaining and building a relationship with major customers is made (and may be linked to the overall marketing plan).

▶ A programme of regular contacts is scheduled for such customers and efforts made to make this fit the service and communication that the customer wants.

▶ Efforts are made to create a partnership between supplier and customer, with an emphasis on working together rather than simply selling because the two businesses are inherently linked.

This happens in both industrial and consumer markets; indeed, the continuity and nature of communications and contact are crucial to developing any business.

All the points made so far about account management are relevant when a major customer is a regular one, such as a supermarket or a large factory. Other major customers may have a more one-off nature; for example, an organisation selling a water treatment plant to a city does not expect to sell it a second unit soon. This "big-ticket selling" is characterised by long lead times and high unit value.

But some customers are small. Together a lot of small ones may have significant value, but the way they are handled must recognise their nature and the cost of dealing with them; for example, personal visits may not be cost-effective. In these circumstances other methods can be used, including:

▶ telephone contact, particularly to ensure appropriate and timely restocking of a product;

▶ channelling business through a wholesaler;

▶ leaving contact to the customer;

▶ allowing business only through such means as mail order.

Customer relationships

Whatever the precise nature of customers, a dialogue must be created with them which must:

▶ suit the customer;

▶ be cost-effective;

▶ remain active and focus on developing the business.

Marketers talk about "relationship management" as if it was a generic term, but it can take a variety of forms. Amazon and mail-order companies such as Lands' End and Boden have excellent customer relationship management techniques "off the page", though they never meet their individual customers.

Customers are demanding, fickle and sometimes difficult. So customer/supplier relationships must be managed in a way that they like (not simply for the supplier's convenience), attempting to screen out competition and build a strong business relationship. Such relationships are inherently fragile – and customers can and do change to another supplier if they do not feel everything is organised in a way that is best for them.

Customer care

The quality of what is essentially a sales relationship is obviously affected by the service involved and delivered in the course of business being done. Customer service, as customers both anticipate and experience it, is fundamental to marketing success. This process is most often called customer care, and its careful execution – in a way designed to impress customers – provides a significant opportunity to differentiate an organisation from competitors.

Excellence in customer care

It is increasingly difficult for customers to differentiate between the competing products and services available. In many industries, products are essentially similar in terms of design, performance and specification, at least within a given price bracket. This is true of both industrial products and consumer goods. Therefore customers' choices will often be influenced as much by subjective considerations as anything else. The nature of customer service can play a crucial role in this, sometimes becoming the most important issue.

The style of customer service adopted becomes an integral part of an organisation's image. Indeed, it should both reflect any existing image and extend it. If a company wants to be seen as efficient, modern and innovative, its customer service must reflect these qualities. A company positioning itself as caring or advisory (in health care or financial services, for example) cannot skimp on time spent with customers without being thought dilatory. Even little things can dilute an image; something as simple as a telephone number is a good example. A number that gets potential customers through to sales is useful, but one that costs them to dial or links them to a labyrinthine system that takes too long to get through may fail to impress. This is certainly true of the impersonal "press 1 for sales, press 2 for customer service" and so on which then puts the caller on hold, and is made worse by the even more irritating (and disingenuous) "your call is important to us, please hold". Even choosing such a simple example makes a point; the greater damage caused by worse mistakes is obvious. Yet sometimes organisations are blind to this and fail to respond to customer enquiries or complaints for months.

Conversely, good customer care is one of the ways to keep customers loyal.

Taking advantage of the opportunity

Any shortfall in prevailing standards presents an opportunity for competitors to steal an edge in the market by getting it right. It is not a question of aiming for perfection (after all, both McDonald's restaurants and the Ritz Hotel would claim to offer good service, but in very different ways). But any organisation must act positively to achieve the standards it has decided its customers require.

What creates good customer care? The answer is primarily the careful consideration of both staffing and organisation. The mix of characteristics and considerations that can help make success more likely is not easily defined. What is certain is that customers know all too well what they like – and do not like – when they encounter it.

Handling complaints

The first task is to minimise the number of complaints received. Every organisation will receive some, but everything that can give rise to them – the product or service, customer service and such things as delivery, policy and people – must be examined to make sure that no complaints occur (especially repeatedly) that could be avoided. Complaints are a source of useful feedback, so they should not be fielded and forgotten. Organisations must learn from them to make improvements. Simple feedback and reporting systems may be required, collecting and centralising data so that it can be analysed and lead to positive action to make improvements. Complaints must be handled in the right way to create a positive out of a negative.

What customers want

The mnemonic PERFECT, much favoured by trainers, summarises what all customer contact must be:

▶ Polite. This almost goes without saying. It reflects the nature of the customer relationship with a supplier and must be manifest throughout the process of communication. Politeness must be genuine. Grovelling will produce the reverse of the desired effect, but a pleasant, personal touch will enhance it. And it must be maintained whatever the circumstances and the pressures.

▶ Efficient. Things must be done properly (and promptly) and that means manifestly for the customer's convenience, not to fit in with an organisation's systems, particularly bureaucratic ones.

▶ Respectful. This is important and must match the customer; some want this much in evidence, others less so, but it must always be there. (An understanding of customers' attitudes to time is a good example: do they want everything done in a moment because they are in a hurry, or do they see time being spent helping them as indicating thoroughness?)

▶ Friendly. The level must be judged just right. Not every customer wants too much too soon, though everyone wants the transaction to be pleasant.

▶ Enthusiastic. This displays an interest in the customer, something most regard as a prerequisite for good customer care.

▶ Cheerful. Even in the face of adversity – no customer wants to feel that the business of being dealt with is getting someone down.

▶ Tactful. Many customer situations have aspects that are confidential or sensitive and respect for them is appreciated.

This sums up the style of handling that works best; the final trick is to apply it individually. Customers like to be dealt with as individuals for the good reason that it is what they are. Anything that seems like a standard approach – dealing with them on "automatic pilot" – dilutes the good customer contact can do. Many customer contact staff wear name badges and some go further: some Häagen-Dazs outlets distribute cards with the name and details of the manager, even including a home telephone number. This is truly a people area of marketing; as a Chinese proverb says: "If you cannot smile, do not open a shop."

Creating good customer care

Creating opportunities to do things better than competitors and gain an edge is very much part of marketing. Excellence of customer care does not just happen – someone must manage the process and the people involved. This must be done at a suitable level and in a way that sees the broad picture and moves towards a vision of how things should be, rather than fire fighting.

In one company, for instance, sales office staff spent time handling complaints about delivery on 75% of orders placed. This was not because delivery was bad, but because members of the sales force – intent on impressing customers and getting orders – were quoting delivery in six weeks when everyone in the company knew it was normally eight weeks. This demonstrates the need to be honest with customers and avoid doing things with the best of intentions so far as the business is concerned that only create problems for it. Such unnecessarily wasted time could have been used more constructively to increase sales, and the action that caused it probably lost the business repeat sales.

Back-up activities to support sales and service

Sales and service staff may succeed or fail largely through their own personal approaches, but they are dependent on the quality of the product they sell and the image of the company for which they sell it. If a job is involved with anything to do with either, people can help to influence sales success.

This is not just to say that those on the production line are involved; there are many more specific circumstances. Examples of people within an organisation who might feel they have little or no relationship with marketing include those:

▶ in technical support, handling a customer query, who will not only sort out the problem, but also influence the likelihood of a customer reordering;

▶ responsible for originating a computer system which, ultimately, interfaces with customers and will affect company image and thus the sales person's relationship with customers;

▶ in accounts, communicating with customers to sort out some invoicing detail, which will affect the image of the company for good or ill.

Every organisation must consider what is done actively to impress customers and what danger areas might create problems for customers. Those outside the marketing department must play their part in minimising the risk of customers experiencing problems.

A marketing oriented organisation loses no opportunity to maximise the positive impressions given by both customer care and sales. The two overlap and both can act to make marketing better able to fulfil its intentions.

Key points

Significant parts of the marketing process are highly personal; overall marketing and promotional activity can only achieve so much. This means:

▶ for many organisations, personal selling is a prime element in the marketing mix;

▶ selling, which involves its own body of techniques, must be well conducted and the people doing it must be skilful and well managed;

▶ customers are not all the same – major customers in particular need special attention, and tailored tactics must be used to develop their business;

▶ all customers, however, expect good service and although this is chronologically well down the chain of marketing events, it is also fundamental. Good service can create customer loyalty and poor or bad service can guarantee that customers vote with their feet and never order again.

Sales and service both contribute to making marketing work. Even a company with little direct contact with its customers must recognise this. As Jeff Bezos, the founder of Amazon, says: "We look for people who have a natural inclination to be intensely focused on the customer." Marketing success is in the details.

Conclusion

Marketing is much too important to leave to the marketing department ... In a truly great marketing organisation, you can't tell who's in the marketing department. Everyone in the organisation has to make decisions based on the impact on the customer.

David Packard, co-founder, Hewlett-Packard

The complexity of marketing is apparent from even a rudimentary examination of what is involved. This book has explained something of the world of marketing and its activities and made clear the logic of its component parts and how they work to create a coherent whole. The starting point is the three Ps – product, price and presentation – together with the fourth P – place.

Given the nature of marketing, it is useful to end on a note linked to the core concept. Five overall factors summarise the essence of what is crucial to marketing success. These can be called the "five Cs" and they apply both to individual aspects of marketing and to its overall operation and success:

▶ Customer. Every aspect of marketing – from concept and planning through to research, communications and the application of every technique – must focus on the customer. "The customer is king", as the saying has it, and ultimately also pays the piper and calls the tune.

▶ Continuous. Marketing is not an option, a bolt-on activity, or for

moments when time allows. It must be present all the time as an
organisation goes about its business. Indeed, without marketing
there is a good chance it will not go about its business, at least
not for long.

▶ Co-ordinated. If the many techniques of marketing do not act
together, their effectiveness will be diluted. For example, sales
and advertising, to pick two obvious factors, are not alternatives;
it is likely that both are necessary in different measure, as are
other techniques and activities. When, how and how much
all these interrelate and overlap is down to the skill of those
involved. Often this co-ordination is made more difficult by
the number of people involved, usually spread across many
departments and sometimes spread throughout the world. The
scale can be huge. For instance, Hilton has some 2,000 hotels
in more than 20 countries, and accommodates 10m guests
each year. On this sort of scale, marketing has to be truly a
management function.

▶ Creativity. Whatever else it must do, marketing must differentiate,
and in what seem to be ever more competitive times this is a
challenging task. It is this combination of competitiveness and
creativity that makes marketing so dynamic. It is not an exact
science, and many of the variables are external. It can never be
known, for instance, what a competitor will do next. So however
the necessary creativity shows itself, through product innovation,
clever (or more important, persuasive and memorable)
advertising or special attention to some aspect of service, it must
always be present, bringing something new to bear to combat
unpredictable competitive pressures. Events breed creativity and
anything new is quickly turned to marketing advantage. A recent
example is reverse graffiti, cleaning defaced walls so that the
clean space creates a message, a word or a logo perhaps. Early
users include Smirnoff and Microsoft.

▶ Culture. Marketing, above all, depends on people. Not only the
people in marketing – the researchers, the marketing and brand
managers, sales managers and account executives – but also the
many others throughout an organisation who are involved in
the process on some way. Some are obvious, such as those in

customer care, and anyone who handles a customer enquiry (or complaint) or provides information, technical support or after sales service contributes. Others are more removed, but can still contribute. Senior managers should not only recognise this, but also work to make sure that everyone contributes knowingly and positively; better still, that as they do so they understand why and get satisfaction from the contribution they are able to make.

The starting point is an understanding of the organisation and its customers in a marketing context and how this affects each individual. Ultimately, a marketing oriented culture can help to generate success and produce the financial strength (for many this is profit) that pays people's salaries and this can only ever come from the market outside the organisation. All five Cs are equally important for all kinds of organisations and the various products and services they provide.

Marketing is a complex and creative process which must be applied to fit individual businesses. But marketing is also a process that ranges wide, that influences the overall success of any organisation that stands or falls on its relationship with the market. As Bruce Henderson, founder of the Boston Consulting Group, says:

Unless a business has a unique advantage over its rivals, it has no reason to exist.

It is that unique advantage that marketing must create. Marketing is a process that is inherently linked to almost every other aspect of an organisation. As such, marketing presents opportunities that affect many people, and many people can have an influence on it and on its ultimate degree of success.

Index

the life and death of
products 17-18
social and ethical
considerations 19-21
market segmentation 21-5
action related to market
segmentation 23-4
how segmentation helps
24-5
size matters 21
what is a market? 21-3
key points 25
Marketing Research Association
60
marketing services 34-5
marketing strategy 95-109
analysis as the basis of
strategic planning 102-6
SWOT analysis 102-6
using the information 106
a basis for success 95-101
the market 96-8
marketing objectives and
strategies 98-101
product life-cycle 101
the scope of planning 106-9
how planning can create
positive change 108
planning to protect
and increase customer
profitability 107-9
key points 109
marketing-led approach to
business 10
market(s) 133
analysis of 117
concentrated 97
the concept of "market" 96-7
definitions 21-3
developing new markets for
existing products/services
98, 115
differentiated 97
expanding existing 115
market types 97-8
mass 22
niche 21, 35, 100
qualitative structure 105
quantitative structure 105
and selection of tactics 119
SOHO market (small office:
home office) 32-3
target 21, 34, 36
test 101
undifferentiated 97
Marlboro cowboy 162
Marriott Hotels 170
Mars 29, 143
mass marketing 23
media 30, 34, 58, 133, 134, **142**
advertising media and
methods 157-9
choosing 187-8
relations 154
Mercedes 33
merchandising 6, 84, 148, 167
assistance 107, 117
spin-offs 143
techniques 11
see also under marketing
communications
Merck 15
methods of payment for
purchases 143
Microsoft 178, 207
mission statements 113-14

SOHO market (small office:
home office) 32-3
Sony 30, 183
Walkman 54
Southwest Airlines 47
spam 166
special editions 170
special offers 38
specialist advice **141**
specialist agencies 34-5
sponsorship 148
staff *see under* labour
stakeholders 152
standards 60, 104, 120, 125
diagnostic 127
moving 127
Starbucks 96, 175
Stella Artois 49
stock levels 170
store cards 169
strategy *see* marketing strategy
strengths and weaknesses
of the organisation 112, 116
of product/service 120
success 2, 7, 104, 208
and distribution 9
impact of distribution on
marketing success 73
marketing influences the
success of any organisation
1
and marketing planning 124
research as a generator of
67-8
use of techniques to make it
more certain 7
Sunkist Growers 146
suppliers 152

supply: a crucial factor 15
supply chain management 89
surveys
and desk research 59-60
planning market research 59
postal 62-3
suspects 137, 138, 138
Swatch 16, 116
switchboard, quality of 151
SWOT analysis (strengths and
weaknesses, opportunities
and threats) 102-6, 115, 119
market opportunities and
threats 105
an organisation's strengths
and weaknesses 103-4
systematic review 133-4

T
tactics
analysing available tactics 118
communications 133
and cost-effectiveness 118
mix of 118
selection of 119-20
tailor-made promotions 171
takeover 99
target audience/market 21, 90,
119, 120, 152-3
taxation, direct/indirect 16
"technical" information 156
technical support 204
technological extension 99
technology 15, 133, 178, 183
telephone interviewing 62
telephoning prospects 193
television advertising 30, 101,
158